Delicious
WAYS TO CONTROL
Diabetes
C O O K B O O K
BOOK 3

Turkey Enchiladas, page 137

Strawberry Shortcakes, page 47

Delicious

WAYS TO CONTROL

Diabetes

C O O K B O O K

BOOK 3

Oxmoor
House®

©2001 by Oxmoor House, Inc.
Book Division of Southern Progress Corporation
P.O. Box 2463, Birmingham, Alabama 35201

ISBN: 0-8487-2396-1
ISSN: 1523-8032
Printed in the United States of America
First Printing 2001

Be sure to check with your health-care provider
before making any changes in your diet.

Editor-in-Chief: Nancy Fitzpatrick Wyatt
Senior Foods Editor: Katherine M. Eakin
Senior Editor, Editorial Services: Olivia Kindig Wells
Art Director: James Boone

Delicious Ways to Control Diabetes Cookbook, Book 3

Editor: Anne Chappell Cain, M.S., M.P.H., R.D.
Associate Art Director: Cynthia R. Cooper
Copy Editor: L. Amanda Owens
Editorial Assistant: Heather Averett
Director, Test Kitchens: Elizabeth Tyler Luckett
Assistant Director, Test Kitchens: Julie Christopher
Recipe Editor: Gayle Hays Sadler
Test Kitchens Staff: Jennifer Cofield; Gretchen Feldtman, R.D.;
    David Gallent; Ana Kelly; Jan A. Smith
Senior Photographer: Jim Bathie
Photographer: Brit Huckabay
Additional photography: Ralph Anderson
Senior Photo Stylist: Kay E. Clarke
Director, Production and Distribution: Phillip Lee
Associate Production Manager: Larry Hunter
Production Assistant: Faye Porter Bonner

Contributors:
Designer: Carol O. Loria
Indexer: Mary Ann Laurens
Photo Stylist: Melanie Clarke
Medical Advisor: David D. DeAtkine, Jr., M.D.

Cover: Fudgy Cream Cheese Brownies, page 60

Contents

Dear Friends,

When you have diabetes, there's no need to end your love affair with food—but you might need to redefine the relationship. I've had diabetes since I was 12 years old, and although my tastes have changed, my enjoyment of eating has not. It really is possible to discover a whole world of wonderful new flavors and tastes, and still keep your diabetes under control.

With Book 3 in the *Delicious Ways to Control Diabetes* series, we want to help you enjoy all of your favorite foods by offering a variety of wonderful dishes that will please you and your entire family.

There is no love sincerer than the love of food.

George Bernard Shaw

Our staff of registered dietitians and cooking experts make sure that each recipe in the book is not only delicious, but also diabetes-approved. Each recipe has nutrient information and exchanges, so whether you use exchanges, count carbohydrates, or are just cutting down on sugar, these recipes will work for you. We've also put together a week of menus so that you can fit these recipes into your family meal plan.

Our readers tell us how much they need quick and easy recipes, so we continue to include recipes that are quick, recipes you can make ahead, and recipes with short ingredient lists.

After you review the recipes, take a look at the 2001 Update to find out about exciting new developments in diabetes management, including news about two new sweeteners on the market. Then turn to the Sugar Substitute Guide on page 10 to see which sugar substitutes are best for your needs.

As you select your favorite recipes, learn from the helpful tips, and sigh over the beautiful food photographs, my hope is that your love of food will be stronger and your increased knowledge will lead to better control of your diabetes.

Sincerely,

Anne Cain

Anne Cain, Editor

2001 UPDATE

The Year's Best News for People with Diabetes

*Until there's a cure, here's some of the best news
we've heard this year about diabetes.*

Need Answers? Log On!

Parents of children with diabetes can find valuable on-line advice and support at the Web site **www.childrenwithdiabetes.com**. Jeff Hitchcock of Hamilton, Ohio, began the site so that he, his wife, and their daughter—who has Type 1 diabetes—could communicate with other families with diabetes.

A team of 30 experts answer health and parenting questions; 5,500 answers are posted on the site for immediate reference. The site also includes a comprehensive list of camps for children with diabetes and a database on school glucose testing policies.

Children with Diabetes delivers a million pages of information each month to families around the world dealing with diabetes. For more information, visit their site.

Eat Your Oatmeal

A diet including plenty of whole-grain products may reduce the risk of Type 2 diabetes. Helpful foods include:

- whole-grain breakfast cereals
- whole-grain bread
- brown rice
- oatmeal

The Harvard Medical School study analyzed the eating habits of more than 75,000 women aged 38 to 63 over a 10-year period. Women whose diets were rich in whole-grain foods had a significantly lower risk of developing diabetes than those whose diets were high in refined-grain products such as pasta, white bread, pizza, cakes, and desserts.

More Fingertip Freedom

An improvement to the LifeScan ONE TOUCH® FastTake® Blood Glucose Monitoring System makes it possible to test using blood samples obtained from the arm rather than the more sensitive fingertips.

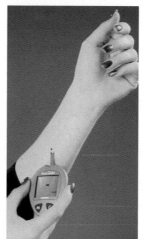

A new test strip for the system requires a 40% smaller blood sample than the original FastTake strip. Because only a tiny drop of blood is required, an adequate sample can be obtained from the arm, which has fewer nerve endings. In test groups, 3 out of 4 patients reported that arm testing was easier and less painful.

The FastTake System also features 15-second test results, a 150-test memory, and automatic 14-day averaging of blood glucose results. For more information, visit **www.LifeScan.com** or call **800-227-8862**.

• •

Closer to a Cure

In a development the Juvenile Diabetes Research Foundation calls **"a significant step forward in curing Type 1 diabetes,"** a research team has succeeded in transplanting pancreatic islet cells into patients with diabetes.

A research team from the University of Alberta, Edmonton, improved success rates of this procedure dramatically in two ways:

• by using a combination of new antirejection drugs.
• by using a larger number of islet cells for each procedure.

In a simple nonsurgical procedure, the islet cells were injected into the patient's portal vein. The cells traveled to the liver and immediately began producing insulin. Patients with the transplants have been able to stop insulin therapy, although they must take antirejection drugs.

Although researchers still don't know what the long-term effects of the antirejection drugs are or how to obtain enough donor islet cells, the results of this study hold great promise. In 10 research centers worldwide, trials have begun using the Edmonton protocol in additional patients.

More $$$ for Diabetes

Federal legislation approved December 15, 2000, calls for increases in Type 1 diabetes research funding at the National Institutes of Health (NIH) from an estimated $134 million in fiscal year 2000 to approximately $220 million in fiscal year 2001, a boost of well over 60 percent.

The move extends the NIH's special juvenile diabetes (Type 1) research program (created in 1997) through 2003 and increases its funding from $30 million per year to $100 million per year.

According to Peter Van Etten, president and CEO of the Juvenile Diabetes Research Foundation International (JDRF), "This legislation marks the most important federal effort ever to combat juvenile diabetes and, along with the dramatic research findings we have seen this year, it could be the turning point in the effort to find a cure."

SWEETENING GETS EASIER

Two sugar substitutes are giving people with diabetes more choices for replacing sugar in their diets.

Sucralose—brand name **Splenda**—is now available in grocery stores nationwide. Sucralose is made from a sugar molecule, but the molecule is rearranged in such a way that keeps it from being broken down by the body. Because it is not broken down, this sweetener is calorie free and does not affect blood glucose levels.

Splenda tolerates heat well, so you can use it in cooking and baking. For more information, call 800-777-5363 or go to www.SPLENDA.com.

Another new sweetener is **DiabetiSweet**. It's made from a combination of acesulfame-K and isomalt. Acesulfame-K is a noncaloric sweetener already on the market (Sunett); isomalt is a mixture of two sugar alcohols—mannitol and sorbitol. DiabetiSweet has about 9 calories and 4.4 grams of carbohydrate per teaspoon.

Look for DiabetiSweet in the pharmacy or diabetes care section of Wal-Mart, Kmart, and Walgreen, or go to www.diabeticproducts.com.

SUGAR SUBSTITUTE GUIDE*

Sugar Substitute	Description	Amount to equal ½ cup sugar
The following sugar substitutes are measured like sugar, so when you use them in recipes to replace sugar, you can use the same amount of substitute as you would use of sugar.		
DiabetiSweet	Contains a combination of acesulfame-K and isomalt; no aftertaste; looks like sugar; heat stable	½ cup
Equal Spoonful	Contains aspartame; no aftertaste; loses some sweetness in high heat	½ cup
Splenda	Contains sucralose, a modified sugar molecule that is not absorbed by the body; no aftertaste; extremely heat stable; also available in packets	½ cup
Sugar Twin	Contains saccharin; some aftertaste; heat stable	½ cup
These sugar substitutes are in more concentrated form, so you do not use as much of these as you would use of sugar in order to get the same sweetness.		
Equal for Recipes	Contains aspartame; no aftertaste; the bulk form of Equal packets; loses some sweetness in high heat	3½ teaspoons
Equal Packets	Contains aspartame; no aftertaste; same as Equal for Recipes, but in packets; loses some sweetness in high heat	12 packets
Sweet 'N Low	Contains saccharin; some aftertaste; available in bulk form or in packets; heat stable	1 tablespoon or 12 packets
Sweet One	Contains acesulfame-K; no aftertaste; heat stable	12 packets
Liquid sugar substitutes blend easily with other ingredients and work well in sauces and marinades.		
Sweet 'N Low	Contains saccharin; some aftertaste; heat stable	1 tablespoon
Sweet-10	Contains saccharin; some aftertaste; heat stable	1 tablespoon

*This list includes the sugar substitutes that we use most often in our Test Kitchens. It is not an inclusive list and is not meant as an endorsement of any particular product.

Appetizers & Beverages

Roasted Pepper Dip, page 12

Roasted Pepper Dip

Yield: 2 cups

3	large sweet red peppers
8	sun-dried tomatoes (packed without oil)
¾	cup boiling water
2	tablespoons chopped fresh parsley
1	tablespoon lemon juice
¼	teaspoon salt
¼	teaspoon pepper
1	clove garlic, minced
4	ounces ⅓-less-fat cream cheese (Neufchâtel), cubed and softened
½	cup fat-free sour cream

Cut peppers in half lengthwise; discard seeds and membranes. Place peppers, skin sides up, on a baking sheet; flatten with hand. Broil peppers 5½ inches from heat 15 minutes or until blackened. Place peppers in a zip-top plastic bag, and seal; let stand 15 minutes. Peel and coarsely chop peppers; discard skins.

Combine tomatoes and boiling water in a small bowl; let stand 5 minutes. Drain.

Combine chopped peppers, tomatoes, parsley, and next 6 ingredients in a food processor. Process until smooth. Transfer mixture to a bowl. Serve with breadsticks or raw vegetables (breadsticks and vegetables not included in analysis).

Per Tablespoon:

Calories 16	Fiber 0.2g
Fat 0.9g (sat 0.0g)	Cholesterol 3mg
Protein 0.7g	Sodium 49mg
Carbohydrate 1.2g	Exchange: Free (up to ¼ cup)

(Photograph on page 11)

Spinach con Queso

Yield: 2½ cups

1   (10-ounce) package frozen chopped spinach, thawed
1   (8-ounce) package fat-free cream cheese, softened
1   cup (4 ounces) shredded reduced-fat sharp Cheddar cheese
¼   cup fat-free evaporated milk
2   teaspoons 40%-less-sodium taco seasoning mix
1   (10-ounce) can diced tomatoes and green chiles, drained
Cooking spray

Drain spinach well, pressing between layers of paper towels to remove excess moisture.

Place cream cheese in a large bowl; mash with a fork until smooth. Add spinach, Cheddar cheese, and next 3 ingredients; stir well. Spoon into a 1-quart baking dish coated with cooking spray.

Bake at 400° for 20 minutes or until mixture is bubbly. Serve dip with low-fat tortilla chips or low-fat crackers (chips and crackers not included in analysis).

Per Tablespoon:

Calories 18	**Fiber** 0.2g
Fat 0.6g (sat 0.3g)	**Cholesterol** 3mg
Protein 2.0g	**Sodium** 84mg
Carbohydrate 0.9g	**Exchange:** Free (up to ½ cup)

Layered Pizza Dip

Yield: 12 appetizer servings (serving size: 5 tablespoons)

1 (8-ounce) package fat-free cream cheese product, softened
½ cup fat-free sour cream
⅛ teaspoon garlic powder
⅛ teaspoon ground red pepper
Cooking spray
½ cup no-salt-added tomato sauce
¼ teaspoon dried oregano
⅛ teaspoon garlic powder
⅛ teaspoon onion powder
½ cup chopped frozen artichoke hearts, thawed
¼ cup sliced green onions
¼ cup chopped sweet red pepper
¼ cup sliced ripe olives
½ cup (2 ounces) shredded part-skim mozzarella cheese
½ teaspoon dried Italian seasoning

Combine first 4 ingredients in a small bowl; beat at low speed of an electric mixer until smooth. Spread cream cheese mixture in a 9-inch pieplate coated with cooking spray.

Combine tomato sauce and next 3 ingredients in a small bowl, stirring well. Pour tomato sauce mixture over cream cheese mixture. Layer artichokes and remaining ingredients over tomato sauce. Bake, uncovered, at 350° for 15 to 20 minutes or until thoroughly heated. Serve with low-fat tortilla chips (chips not included in analysis).

Per Serving:

Calories 48	Fiber 0.5g
Fat 1.4g (sat 0.6g)	Cholesterol 6mg
Protein 4.9g	Sodium 189mg
Carbohydrate 3.5g	Exchanges: 1 Vegetable, ½ Very Lean Meat

Southwestern Two-Bean Salsa

Yield: 4 cups

1	(15-ounce) can black-eyed peas, drained
1	(15-ounce) can red beans, drained
1	cup seeded, chopped tomato
⅔	cup salsa
½	cup thinly sliced green onions
⅓	cup chopped fresh cilantro
3	tablespoons fresh lime juice
½	teaspoon ground cumin
2	cloves garlic, minced
1	jalapeño pepper, seeded and chopped

Combine all ingredients in a large bowl, stirring well. Cover and chill at least 2 hours. Serve with low-fat tortilla chips (chips not included in analysis).

Per Tablespoon:

Calories 13	**Fiber** 0.3g
Fat 0.1g (sat 0.0g)	**Cholesterol** 0mg
Protein 0.9g	**Sodium** 48mg
Carbohydrate 2.3g	**Exchange:** Free (up to 3 tablespoons)

Garlic-Cheese Toasts

Yield: 24 appetizers

½ cup ⅓-less-fat cream cheese (Neufchâtel), softened
1½ tablespoons chopped fresh chives
1 tablespoon grated fat-free Parmesan topping
1 clove garlic, minced
24 (½-inch-thick) slices French baguette, toasted

Combine first 4 ingredients in a small bowl, stirring until smooth. Spread 1 teaspoon cream cheese mixture over one side of each toasted baguette slice.

Per Appetizer:

Calories 36	**Fiber** 0.1g
Fat 1.0g (sat 0.5g)	**Cholesterol** 3mg
Protein 1.4g	**Sodium** 79mg
Carbohydrate 5.2g	**Exchange:** ½ Starch

Serve these savory cheese toasts on an appetizer buffet with ham or roast beef. They're also good with soup or as a snack.

Stuffed Cherry Tomatoes

Yield: 20 appetizers

20   large cherry tomatoes
½   cup ⅓-less-fat cream cheese (Neufchâtel)
2   tablespoons fat-free Ranch dressing
4   (½-ounce) slices Canadian bacon, finely chopped
3   tablespoons minced green onions
¼   teaspoon ground white pepper
⅛   teaspoon garlic powder
⅛   teaspoon hot sauce
Parsley sprigs (optional)

Cut top off each tomato; carefully scoop out pulp. Reserve pulp for another use. Invert tomato shells onto paper towels, and let drain 30 minutes.

Combine cream cheese and Ranch dressing, stirring well. Add Canadian bacon and next 4 ingredients; stir well. Spoon mixture evenly into tomato shells, or pipe into shells using a decorating bag fitted with a large round tip. Garnish with parsley, if desired.

Per Appetizer:

Calories 22	**Fiber** 0.2g
Fat 1.2g (sat 0.6g)	**Cholesterol** 5mg
Protein 1.3g	**Sodium** 88mg
Carbohydrate 1.5g	**Exchange:** Free (up to 4 appetizers)

Turkey-Spinach Pinwheels

Yield: 8 appetizer servings (serving size: 4 pinwheels)

½ cup fat-free cream cheese, softened
1 tablespoon pesto
2 teaspoons Dijon mustard
4 (8-inch) fat-free flour tortillas
1 medium tomato, very thinly sliced and seeded (see photo)
12 (½-ounce) slices turkey breast
16 large spinach leaves, stems removed

Combine first 3 ingredients in a small bowl, stirring well. Spread cream cheese mixture evenly over one side of tortillas. Arrange tomato slices evenly over cream cheese mixture; top evenly with turkey and spinach leaves.

Roll up tortillas, jellyroll fashion. Wrap each roll in plastic wrap, and chill at least 1 hour. Remove plastic wrap, and cut each roll into 8 slices.

Per Serving:

Calories 100

Fat 1.2g (sat 0.4g)

Protein 7.2g

Carbohydrate 14.8g

Fiber 1.2g

Cholesterol 8mg

Sodium 432mg

Exchanges: 1 Starch, ½ Lean Meat

Seeding Tomato Slices

Use a spoon to scoop or press out the seeds.

Salsa Meatballs

Yield: 16 appetizer servings
(serving size: 3 meatballs and 1 tablespoon sauce)

1	pound freshly ground raw turkey
½	cup salsa, divided
¼	cup fine, dry breadcrumbs
¼	cup (1 ounce) shredded reduced-fat Monterey Jack cheese
2	tablespoons finely chopped green onions
2	cloves garlic, minced

Cooking spray
¾   cup fat-free sour cream

Combine turkey, ¼ cup salsa, breadcrumbs, and next 3 ingredients in a large bowl; stir well. Shape turkey mixture into 48 (¾-inch) balls. Place meatballs on rack of a broiler pan coated with cooking spray. Bake at 400° for 20 to 25 minutes or until done. Drain on paper towels.

Combine sour cream and remaining ¼ cup salsa, stirring well. Serve meatballs warm with sour cream sauce mixture.

Per Serving:

Calories 57	**Fiber** 0.3g
Fat 1.2g (sat 0.6g)	**Cholesterol** 21mg
Protein 7.8g	**Sodium** 119mg
Carbohydrate 2.7g	**Exchange:** 1 Very Lean Meat

Orange Smoothie

Yield: 6 (1-cup) servings

1	(6-ounce) can frozen orange juice concentrate, thawed
1	cup water
1	cup fat-free milk
¼	cup granulated sugar substitute (such as Sugar Twin)
1	teaspoon vanilla extract
⅛	teaspoon almond extract
4	cups ice cubes

Combine first 6 ingredients in container of an electric blender; top with cover, and process 30 seconds. Gradually add ice cubes, and process until mixture is smooth.

Transfer mixture to a large pitcher. Serve immediately.

Per Serving:

Calories 68	**Fiber** 0.2g
Fat 0.2g (sat 0.1g)	**Cholesterol** 1mg
Protein 2.0g	**Sodium** 32mg
Carbohydrate 14.6g	**Exchange:** 1 Fruit

Bellini Spritzers

Yield: 9 (1-cup) servings

2   pounds medium to large fresh peaches, peeled and halved
1   (750-milliliter) bottle champagne or sparkling white grape juice, chilled
2   cups sparkling mineral water

Place peaches in food processor; cover and process until smooth, stopping once to scrape down sides.

Combine puree, champagne, and mineral water in a large pitcher; stir gently. Pour into chilled glasses. Serve immediately.

Per Serving:

Calories 96	**Fiber** 1.2g
Fat 0.1g (sat 0.0g)	**Cholesterol** 0mg
Protein 0.8g	**Sodium** 14mg
Carbohydrate 9.4g	**Exchange:** 1 Fruit

Use 4 cups frozen sliced peaches, thawed, if fresh peaches are not in season.

Frosted Cappuccino

Yield: 4 (1-cup servings)

2   cups brewed espresso (or very strong brewed coffee), chilled
2   cups vanilla no-added-sugar, fat-free ice cream
½   teaspoon vanilla extract
Ground cinnamon (optional)

Combine first 3 ingredients in container of an electric blender; cover and process until smooth. Pour into glasses. Sprinkle each serving with cinnamon, if desired. Serve immediately.

Per Serving:

Calories 94	**Fiber** 1.0g
Fat 0.0g (sat 0.0g)	**Cholesterol** 0mg
Protein 4.1g	**Sodium** 78mg
Carbohydrate 21.6g	**Exchange:** 1½ Starch

Create the sweet taste and texture of a luxuriously rich coffee beverage without the sugar and fat.

Breads

Buttermilk Corn Sticks, page 34

Garlic Bread

Yield: 16 slices

¼   cup reduced-calorie margarine, softened
¼   cup grated Parmesan cheese
2   cloves garlic, pressed
¼   teaspoon dried marjoram
¼   teaspoon dried oregano
1   (16-ounce) loaf French bread, cut into 16 slices

Combine first 5 ingredients; stir well. Spread mixture evenly between bread slices.

Reassemble loaf, and wrap in heavy-duty aluminum foil; place on a baking sheet.

Bake at 350° for 20 minutes. Open foil, and bake 5 additional minutes or until crisp and golden. Serve immediately.

Per Slice:

Calories 104	**Fiber** 0.7g
Fat 2.8g (sat 0.7g)	**Cholesterol** 2mg
Protein 3.1g	**Sodium** 215mg
Carbohydrate 15.9g	**Exchanges:** 1 Starch, ½ Fat

The margarine mixture is also good as a tasty topping for baked potatoes.

Ready in 15 Minutes!

Herbed Cheese French Bread

Yield: 16 servings

½   cup part-skim ricotta cheese
1   tablespoon chopped fresh parsley or 1 teaspoon dried
           parsley flakes
1   teaspoon minced garlic
½   teaspoon fines herbes
Dash of ground red pepper
2   green onions, chopped
1   (16-ounce) loaf French bread

Combine first 6 ingredients; stir well. Slice bread in half lengthwise. Spread cheese mixture evenly over cut sides of bread; place on a baking sheet.

Broil 5½ inches from heat for 5 minutes or until bread is lightly browned. Serve warm.

Per Serving:

Calories 94	**Fiber** 0.7g
Fat 1.2g (sat 0.6g)	**Cholesterol** 3mg
Protein 3.5g	**Sodium** 175mg
Carbohydrate 16.3g	**Exchange:** 1 Starch

For a quick make-ahead recipe, spread the cheese mixture on the bread, and wrap each loaf half in foil. Store the bread in the freezer. When ready to serve, remove bread from the freezer, unwrap, and place on baking sheet. Bake at 350° for 15 minutes.

Curried Peppercorn Rolls

Yield: 8 rolls

2   tablespoons creamy mustard blend (such as Dijonnaise)
1/2 teaspoon coarsely ground pepper
1/4 teaspoon curry powder
1   (11-ounce) can refrigerated breadstick dough
Cooking spray

Combine first 3 ingredients, stirring well.

Unroll breadstick dough onto work surface, being careful not to separate dough. Spread mustard mixture evenly over dough. Separate dough into 8 strips. Coil each strip of dough into a spiral shape.

Place on a baking sheet coated with cooking spray. Bake at 350° for 16 to 18 minutes or until lightly browned. Serve warm.

Per Roll:

Calories 115	**Fiber** 0.1g
Fat 2.6g (sat 0.5g)	**Cholesterol** 0mg
Protein 3.0g	**Sodium** 343mg
Carbohydrate 18.9g	**Exchanges:** 1 Starch, 1/2 Fat

Beer-Cheese Muffins

Yield: 1½ dozen

2½ cups low-fat biscuit and baking mix
½ cup cornmeal
¾ cup (3 ounces) shredded reduced-fat Cheddar cheese
½ cup chopped green onions (about 2 large)
2 teaspoons dry mustard
1 teaspoon dried dillweed
1 (12-ounce) can light beer
Cooking spray

Combine first 6 ingredients; stir well. Add beer, stirring just until dry ingredients are moistened.

Spoon batter evenly into muffin pans coated with cooking spray, filling two-thirds full. Bake at 375° for 25 minutes or until golden. Remove from pans immediately to keep muffins from sticking. Serve warm.

Per Muffin:

Calories 94	**Fiber** 0.4g
Fat 2.2g (sat 0.8g)	**Cholesterol** 3mg
Protein 3.1g	**Sodium** 230mg
Carbohydrate 15.3g	**Exchanges:** 1 Starch, ½ Fat

The alcohol evaporates as the bread bakes, leaving only the flavor of the beer.

Blueberry Bran Muffins

Yield: 16 muffins

1½   cups all-purpose flour
½   cup unprocessed wheat bran
2   teaspoons baking powder
¼   teaspoon salt
¾   cup sugar
¾   cup fat-free milk
2   tablespoons vegetable oil
1   egg, lightly beaten
1   teaspoon vanilla extract
1½   cups fresh or frozen blueberries, thawed
Cooking spray

Combine first 5 ingredients in a medium bowl; make a well in center of mixture.

Combine milk and next 3 ingredients; add to dry ingredients, stirring just until dry ingredients are moistened. Fold in blueberries.

Spoon batter into muffin pans coated with cooking spray, filling two-thirds full. Bake at 400° for 18 to 20 minutes or until golden. Remove from pans immediately to keep muffins from sticking. Serve warm.

Per Muffin:

Calories 118	**Fiber** 1.8g
Fat 2.5g (sat 0.5g)	**Cholesterol** 14mg
Protein 2.4g	**Sodium** 48mg
Carbohydrate 22.4g	**Exchanges:** 1 Starch, ½ Fruit

Popovers

Yield: 8 popovers

1   cup bread flour
1   cup 1% low-fat milk
¾   cup fat-free egg substitute
1   tablespoon sugar
1   tablespoon vegetable oil
¼   teaspoon salt
Cooking spray

Combine first 6 ingredients in food processor bowl. Process until smooth, stopping once to scrape down sides.

Pour batter into popover pans coated with cooking spray, filling one-half full. Place in a cold oven. Turn oven on 450°, and bake 15 minutes. Reduce heat to 350°, and bake 35 to 40 additional minutes or until popovers are crusty and brown.

Per Popover:

Calories 109	**Fiber** 0.4g
Fat 2.5g (sat 0.6g)	**Cholesterol** 1mg
Protein 5.3g	**Sodium** 123mg
Carbohydrate 15.9g	**Exchanges:** 1 Starch, ½ Fat

For an easy variation, stir ½ teaspoon dried dillweed and ⅛ teaspoon onion powder into the flour mixture, and proceed with the recipe as directed. The nutrient values and exchanges will be the same for both versions.

What hymns are sung and praises said
for the home-made miracle of bread?

LOUIS UNTERNEYER, American Writer

bread

Buttermilk Corn Sticks

Yield: 1 dozen

⅔	cup yellow cornmeal
½	cup all-purpose flour
¾	teaspoon baking powder
½	teaspoon baking soda
¼	teaspoon salt
¼	teaspoon paprika
¾	cup fat-free or low-fat buttermilk
2	tablespoons sugar
2	tablespoons vegetable oil
1	egg, lightly beaten

Cooking spray

Combine first 6 ingredients in a medium bowl; make a well in center of mixture.

Combine buttermilk and next 3 ingredients; add to dry ingredients, stirring just until moistened.

Place cast-iron corn stick pans coated with cooking spray in a 425° oven for 3 minutes or until hot. Remove pans from oven; spoon batter into pans, filling two-thirds full. Bake at 425° for 10 minutes or until lightly browned.

Per Corn Stick:

Calories 88	**Fiber** 0.5g
Fat 3.0g (sat 0.6g)	**Cholesterol** 19mg
Protein 2.3g	**Sodium** 124mg
Carbohydrate 13.0g	**Exchanges:** 1 Starch, ½ Fat

(Photograph on page 25)

Chile-Cheese Cornbread

Yield: 16 servings

1   cup yellow cornmeal
1   cup all-purpose flour
1   tablespoon plus 1 teaspoon baking powder
¼   teaspoon salt
¼   fat-free dry milk powder
1   tablespoon sugar
1   cup cold water
½   cup fat-free egg substitute
2   tablespoons vegetable oil
¾   cup (3 ounces) shredded reduced-fat Cheddar cheese
1   (4-ounce) can chopped green chiles, drained
Cooking spray

Combine first 6 ingredients in a medium bowl; make a well in center of mixture.

Combine water, egg substitute, and oil; add to dry ingredients, stirring just until dry ingredients are moistened. Stir in cheese and green chiles.

Pour batter into an 8-inch square baking dish coated with cooking spray. Bake at 375° for 30 minutes or until cornbread is golden.

Per Serving:

Calories 107	**Fiber** 0.7g
Fat 3.0g (sat 0.9g)	**Cholesterol** 4mg
Protein 4.6g	**Sodium** 125mg
Carbohydrate 15.3g	**Exchange:** 1 Starch

Strawberry Bread

Yield: 14 (½-inch) slices

1½ cups all-purpose flour
½ teaspoon baking soda
¼ teaspoon salt
½ cup sugar
½ teaspoon ground cinnamon
1 egg white, lightly beaten
1 cup frozen unsweetened strawberries, thawed and coarsely
 chopped
2 tablespoons vegetable oil
⅓ cup chopped pecans
Cooking spray

Combine first 5 ingredients in a large bowl; make a well in center of mixture.

Combine egg white, strawberries, and oil, stirring well; add to flour mixture, stirring just until dry ingredients are moistened. Stir in pecans.

Spoon batter into a 7½- x 3-inch loafpan coated with cooking spray. Bake at 350° for 1 hour or until a wooden pick inserted in center comes out clean. Cool in pan 10 minutes. Remove from pan, and let cool completely on a wire rack.

Per Slice:

Calories 116	**Fiber** 0.6g
Fat 3.9g (sat 0.5g)	**Cholesterol** 0mg
Protein 1.9g	**Sodium** 91mg
Carbohydrate 18.8g	**Exchanges:** 1 Starch, 1 Fat

Whole Wheat Biscuits

Yield: 1 dozen

½ cup warm fat-free or low-fat buttermilk (120° to 130°)
1 package rapid-rise yeast
1¾ cups all-purpose flour
¾ cup whole wheat flour
1½ teaspoons baking powder
½ teaspoon baking soda
¼ teaspoon salt
2 teaspoons sugar
3 tablespoons reduced-calorie margarine
½ cup unsweetened applesauce
Cooking spray

Combine buttermilk and yeast in a 1-cup liquid measuring cup; let stand 5 minutes.

Combine all-purpose flour and next 5 ingredients in a large bowl. Cut in margarine with a pastry blender until mixture is crumbly. Add buttermilk mixture and applesauce to flour mixture, stirring just until dry ingredients are moistened.

Turn dough out onto a lightly floured surface, and knead gently 3 or 4 times. Roll dough to ½-inch thickness; cut into rounds with a 2½-inch biscuit cutter. Place rounds on a baking sheet coated with cooking spray; cover and let rise in a warm place (85°), free from drafts, 10 minutes. Bake at 400° for 10 to 12 minutes. Serve warm.

Per Biscuit:

Calories 120	**Fiber** 1.8g
Fat 2.2g (sat 0.3g)	**Cholesterol** 0mg
Protein 3.5g	**Sodium** 213mg
Carbohydrate 22.1g	**Exchanges:** 1½ Starch, ½ Fat

Bread is like dresses, hats, and shoes—in other words, essential!

EMILY POST, American etiquette authority

Parmesan Breadsticks

Yield: 32 breadsticks

1   (16-ounce) package hot roll mix
¼   cup grated Parmesan cheese
1   cup hot water (120° to 130°)
1   egg white, lightly beaten
2   tablespoons vegetable oil
1   teaspoon dried Italian seasoning
Butter-flavored cooking spray
2   tablespoons plus 2 teaspoons grated Parmesan cheese

Combine roll mix, yeast from packet, and ¼ cup cheese in a bowl. Add hot water and next 3 ingredients; stir until moistened. Shape dough into a ball. Turn dough out onto a lightly floured surface; knead until smooth and elastic (about 5 minutes). Cover; let rest 5 minutes.

Roll dough into 16- x 12-inch rectangle on a lightly floured surface. Cut rectangle with a pastry cutter to form 16 strips. Cut 16 strips in half lengthwise to form 32 (6-inch) strips.

Twist each strip 5 or 6 times; place on baking sheets coated with cooking spray. Spray tops of strips with cooking spray; sprinkle each strip with ¼ teaspoon cheese.

Cover; let rise in a warm place (85°), free from drafts, 20 to 30 minutes, or until doubled in bulk. Bake at 375° for 12 minutes or until golden.

Per Breadstick:

Calories 63	**Fiber** 0g
Fat 1.2g (sat 0.4g)	**Cholesterol** 1mg
Protein 2.0g	**Sodium** 121mg
Carbohydrate 10.6g	**Exchange:** 1 Starch

Cherry Coffee Cake

Yield: 12 servings

½   (32-ounce) package frozen bread dough, thawed
Cooking spray
½   cup ⅓-less-fat cream cheese (Neufchâtel), softened
2   tablespoons measure-for-measure sugar substitute
       (such as DiabetiSweet), divided
1   teaspoon vanilla extract
⅓   cup dried cherries
1½ tablespoons honey
1   tablespoon fat-free milk
½   cup measure-for-measure sugar substitute
2   teaspoons fat-free milk
¼   teaspoon vanilla extract

Roll dough into a 12- x 8-inch rectangle on a baking sheet coated with cooking spray. Combine cream cheese, 1 tablespoon sugar substitute, and 1 teaspoon vanilla; stir well. Spoon lengthwise down center third of dough. Sprinkle cherries over cheese mixture; drizzle with honey.

Cut 12 (1-inch-wide) strips from edge of filling to edge of dough on long sides of rectangle. Fold strips, alternating sides, at an angle across filling (see photo). Brush dough with 1 tablespoon milk. Sprinkle with 1 tablespoon sugar substitute. Bake at 375° for 20 minutes or until golden. Combine ½ cup sugar substitute, 2½ teaspoons milk, and ¼ teaspoon vanilla, stirring well; drizzle over warm coffee cake.

Per Serving:

Calories 155
Fat 3.8g (sat 0.0g)
Protein 3.8g
Carbohydrate 32.5g

Fiber 1.3g
Cholesterol 7mg
Sodium 205mg
Exchanges: 1 Starch, 1 Fruit, ½ Fat

Folding Dough Strips

Zesty Orange Bread

Yield: 24 (1-inch) slices

2 to 2½ cups bread flour, divided
1½ cups medium rye flour
1   package rapid-rise yeast
1   teaspoon salt
2   teaspoons orange rind
1½ cups warm orange juice (120° to 130°)
Cooking spray
1   tablespoon cornmeal

Combine 1 cup bread flour, rye flour, and next 3 ingredients in a large bowl; stir well. Add juice to flour mixture, beating well at low speed of an electric mixer. Beat 2 minutes at medium speed. Stir in enough remaining bread flour to make a soft dough.

Turn dough out onto a lightly floured surface; knead until smooth and elastic (about 8 minutes). Cover dough; let rest 10 minutes. Coat baking sheet with cooking spray. Sprinkle with cornmeal. Divide dough in half. Shape each half into an oval loaf. Place loaves on baking sheet. Cover and let rise in a warm place (85°), free from drafts, 30 minutes or until doubled in bulk.

Using a sharp knife, make three slits across top of each loaf. Bake at 375° for 20 minutes or until loaves sound hollow when tapped. Remove loaves from baking sheet immediately; cool on wire racks.

Per Slice:

Calories 74	Fiber 1.3g
Fat 0.3g (sat 0.0g)	Cholesterol 0mg
Protein 2.2g	Sodium 98mg
Carbohydrate 15.6g	Exchange: 1 Starch

Desserts

Mocha Trifle, page 51

Raspberry-Peach Topping

Yield: 14 (¼-cup) servings

2	cups chopped fresh peaches (about 2 large peaches)
1	cup water, divided
½	(12-ounce) can frozen apple juice concentrate, thawed
3	tablespoons cornstarch
¼	teaspoon almond extract
1	cup fresh raspberries

Combine chopped peaches, ⅔ cup water, and juice concentrate in a medium saucepan; cook over medium heat 5 minutes or until peaches are tender.

Combine cornstarch and remaining ⅓ cup water; stir into peach mixture. Bring to a boil; cook, stirring constantly, 1 minute or until mixture is thickened and bubbly. Remove from heat; stir in almond extract. Cool completely. Stir in raspberries before serving. Serve over angel food cake or fat-free pound cake (cake not included in analysis).

Per Serving:

Calories 44	**Fiber** 1.1g
Fat 0.1g (sat 0.0g)	**Cholesterol** 0mg
Protein 0.4g	**Sodium** 3mg
Carbohydrate 10.9g	**Exchange:** ½ Fruit

A 1-ounce slice of angel food cake or fat-free pound cake has about 16 to 17 grams of carbohydrate and counts as 1 Starch exchange.

Fresh Berries with Creamy Peach Topping

Yield: 6 (⅔-cup) servings

1	cup sliced fresh or frozen peaches, thawed
¼	cup low-fat sour cream
1	tablespoon granulated brown sugar substitute (such as brown Sugar Twin)
½	teaspoon lemon juice
3	cups fresh strawberry halves
1	cup fresh blackberries

Combine first 4 ingredients in container of an electric blender; cover and process until smooth.

Spoon ⅔ cup berries into each of 6 dessert dishes. Spoon peach mixture evenly over berries.

Per Serving:

Calories 61	**Fiber** 3.6g
Fat 1.6g (sat 0.8g)	**Cholesterol** 4mg
Protein 1.1g	**Sodium** 7mg
Carbohydrate 11.9g	**Exchange:** 1 Fruit

Strawberry Shortcakes

Yield: 6 servings (serving size: 1 cake and ⅓ cup sauce)

1	tablespoon granulated sugar substitute (such as Splenda)
1	tablespoon cornstarch
1	cup orange juice
¼	teaspoon vanilla or almond extract
1½	cups sliced fresh strawberries (about 1 pint)
6	spongecake dessert shells (5-ounce package)

Combine sugar substitute and cornstarch in a small saucepan. Stir in orange juice. Bring to a boil; cook, stirring constantly, 1 minute or until mixture is thickened and bubbly. Remove from heat, and stir in extract. Cool completely.

Combine orange juice mixture and strawberries in a bowl; stir gently. Cover and chill 30 minutes.

To serve, spoon sauce over dessert shells.

Per Serving:

Calories 113	**Fiber** 0.2g
Fat 0.9g (sat 0.3g)	**Cholesterol** 33mg
Protein 2.0g	**Sodium** 169mg
Carbohydrate 24.3g	**Exchanges:** 1 Starch, ½ Fruit

This luscious sauce is also good spooned over no-sugar-added ice cream, angel food cake, or fat-free pound cake.

Blessed be he that invented pudding,
for it is a Manna that hits the Palates
of all Sorts of People.

FRANÇOISE MAXIMILIEN MISSION, French writer

Peanut Butter-Banana Pudding

Yield: 12 servings (serving size: about 1 cup)

1   (1-ounce) package vanilla sugar-free, fat-free instant pudding mix
2   cups fat-free milk
⅓   cup no-added-sugar creamy peanut butter (such as Fifty-50)
1   (8-ounce) carton fat-free sour cream
42   vanilla wafers, divided
6   small bananas, divided
1   (8-ounce) carton frozen fat-free whipped topping, thawed
1   tablespoon lemon juice

Prepare pudding mix according to package directions, using a whisk and 2 cups fat-free milk. (Do not use an electric mixer.) Add peanut butter and sour cream, stirring well with a wire whisk.

Line bottom of a 2½-quart casserole with 14 vanilla wafers. Peel and slice 4 bananas. Top wafers with one-third each of pudding mixture, banana slices, and whipped topping. Repeat layers twice using remaining wafers, pudding mixture, banana, and topping. Cover and chill at least 2 hours. Peel and slice remaining 2 bananas; toss with lemon juice. Arrange slices around outer edges of dish.

Per Serving:

Calories 236	**Fiber** 1.9g
Fat 7.4g (sat 0.9g)	**Cholesterol** 1mg
Protein 6.1g	**Sodium** 230mg
Carbohydrate 36.0g	**Exchanges:** 2 Starch, ½ Fruit, 1 Fat

Banana Cream Pie

Yield: 8 servings

1   (0.9-ounce) package banana sugar-free, fat-free instant pudding mix
1   cup 1% low-fat milk
1¾   cups frozen reduced-calorie whipped topping, thawed and divided
1¼   cups peeled, sliced banana (about 2 medium)
1   tablespoon lemon juice
1   (6-ounce) chocolate graham cracker crust

Combine pudding mix and milk in a medium bowl, stirring with a wire whisk until smooth. Gently fold 1 cup whipped topping into pudding mixture.

Toss banana slices with lemon juice. Arrange banana slices over crust. Spoon pudding mixture over banana. Cover and chill 1½ hours or until set. Pipe or spoon remaining ¾ cup whipped topping around edge of pie just before serving.

Per Serving:

Calories 182	**Fiber** 0.6g
Fat 6.8g (sat 2.1g)	**Cholesterol** 1mg
Protein 3.0g	**Sodium** 310mg
Carbohydrate 28.0g	**Exchanges:** 1 Starch, 1 Fruit, 1 Fat

Mocha Trifle

Yield: 16 (¾-cup) servings

1   (2.1-ounce) package chocolate sugar-free, fat-free instant pudding mix
3   cups fat-free milk
1   (15-ounce) loaf fat-free chocolate pound cake
      (such as Entennman's)
½   cup strong brewed coffee, divided
1   (8-ounce) carton frozen fat-free whipped topping, thawed
½   (7.25-ounce) package sugar-free chocolate sandwich cookies,
      chopped (such as Fifty-50)

Prepare pudding mix according to package directions, using 3 cups fat-free milk.

Cut cake into cubes; place half of cake cubes in a 3-quart trifle bowl or glass bowl. Pour ¼ cup coffee over cake; top with half of pudding, whipped topping, and chopped cookies. Repeat layers. Cover and chill at least 4 hours.

Per Serving:

Calories 148	**Fiber** 0.8g
Fat 1.4g (sat 0.4g)	**Cholesterol** 1mg
Protein 3.1g	**Sodium** 303mg
Carbohydrate 29.3g	**Exchanges:** 2 Starch

(Photograph on page 43)

Cantaloupe Sherbet

Yield: 5 (1-cup) servings

1   large ripe cantaloupe, peeled and finely chopped (about 5 cups)
⅓   cup granulated sugar substitute with aspartame (such as Equal
       Spoonful)
2   tablespoons lemon juice
2   teaspoons unflavored gelatin
¼   cup cold water
1   (8-ounce) carton vanilla fat-free yogurt sweetened with aspartame
Cantaloupe wedge (optional)

Combine cantaloupe, sugar substitute, and lemon juice in container of an electric blender or food processor; cover and process until smooth. Transfer mixture to a medium bowl.

Sprinkle gelatin over cold water in a small saucepan; let stand 1 minute. Cook over low heat, stirring until gelatin dissolves, about 4 minutes. Add to cantaloupe mixture, stirring well. Add yogurt, stirring until smooth.

Pour mixture into an 8-inch square pan; freeze until almost firm. Transfer mixture to a large bowl; beat at high speed of an electric mixer until fluffy. Spoon mixture back into pan; freeze until firm. Scoop into individual serving dishes to serve. Garnish each serving with a cantaloupe wedge, if desired.

Per Serving:

Calories 93	**Fiber** 1.3g
Fat 0.5g (sat 0.2g)	**Cholesterol** 1mg
Protein 5.1g	**Sodium** 50mg
Carbohydrate 18.9g	**Exchanges:** 1 Fruit, ½ Skim Milk

Rocky Road Fudge Pops

Yield: 12 pops

1   (1.4-ounce) package chocolate sugar-free, fat-free instant
         pudding mix
2   tablespoons granulated sugar substitute (such as Sugar Twin)
1   cup fat-free milk
1   (12-ounce) can fat-free evaporated milk
¾   cup miniature marshmallows
⅓   cup chopped sugar-free milk chocolate bar (2 ounces)
¼   cup plus 3 tablespoons coarsely chopped unsalted dry roasted
         peanuts, divided

Combine pudding mix and sugar substitute in a large bowl.
Gradually add fat-free milk and evaporated milk, stirring with
a wire whisk until smooth. Stir in marshmallows, chocolate,
and ¼ cup peanuts.

Sprinkle remaining 3 tablespoons peanuts evenly among 12 plastic
holders. Pour pudding mixture into holders, and add sticks. Freeze
3 hours or until firm.

Per Pop:

Calories 107	**Fiber** 0.7g
Fat 4.2g (sat 1.2g)	**Cholesterol** 2mg
Protein 4.6g	**Sodium** 157mg
Carbohydrate 13.6g	**Exchanges:** 1 Starch, ½ Fat

Look for the plastic holders at specialty kitchen
shops, or use 3-ounce paper cups and craft
sticks.

Blueberry Pound Cake

Yield: 18 servings

2   cups plus 6 tablespoons DiabetiSweet sugar substitute, divided
1/3   cup stick margarine, softened
1/2   cup (4 ounces) 1/3-less-fat cream cheese, softened
3   large eggs
1   large egg white
2   teaspoons vanilla extract
3   cups all-purpose flour, divided
2   cups fresh or frozen blueberries
1   teaspoon baking powder
1/2   teaspoon baking soda
1/2   teaspoon salt
1   (8-ounce) carton lemon low-fat yogurt
Cooking spray
1 1/2 tablespoons lemon juice

Beat 2 cups sugar substitute, margarine, and cream cheese with a mixer until blended. Add eggs and egg white, one at a time, beating after each addition. Beat in vanilla. Combine 2 tablespoons flour and blueberries; toss. Combine remaining flour, baking powder, soda, and salt. Add flour mixture to cheese mixture alternately with yogurt. Fold in blueberries. Pour into a 10-inch tube pan coated with cooking spray. Bake at 350° for 1 hour and 5 minutes or until a pick inserted in center comes out clean. Cool in pan 10 minutes on a rack; remove cake from sides of pan. Cool 15 minutes on rack; remove cake from bottom of pan. Combine 6 tablespoons sugar substitute and lemon juice; drizzle over cake.

Per Serving:

Calories 220	**Fiber** 1.0g
Fat 6.5g (sat 2.1g)	**Cholesterol** 47mg
Protein 4.8g	**Sodium** 215mg
Carbohydrate 49.0g	**Exchanges:** 2 Starch, 1 Fruit, 1 Fat

Triple-Chocolate Bundt Cake

Yield: 18 servings

½   cup unsweetened applesauce
1   (18.25-ounce) package devil's food cake mix with pudding
1   (1.4-ounce) package chocolate sugar-free, fat-free pudding mix
1   cup fat-free sour cream
⅓   cup fat-free milk
3   large egg whites
1   large egg
1   teaspoon almond extract
Cooking spray
3   tablespoons Equal Measure or 31 packets Equal
2½ teaspoons fat-free milk
1   ounce sugar-free milk chocolate
1   tablespoon fat-free milk

Spread applesauce onto several layers of paper towels. Cover with additional paper towels; let stand 5 minutes. Scrape into a bowl. Combine cake mix and next 6 ingredients in a large bowl; add applesauce. Beat with a mixer 2 minutes. Pour into a 12-cup Bundt pan coated with cooking spray. Bake at 350° for 53 minutes or until a pick inserted in center comes out clean. Cool in pan on wire rack 10 minutes; remove from pan. Cool completely on wire rack.

Combine sugar substitute and 2½ teaspoons milk; drizzle over cake. Place chocolate in a microwave-safe dish; microwave at HIGH 1½ minutes, stirring after 1 minute. Add 1 tablespoon milk; stir. Drizzle over cake.

Per Serving:

Calories 156

Fat 2.5g (sat 0.4g)

Protein 3.5g

Carbohydrate 29.3g

Fiber 0.7g

Cholesterol 13mg

Sodium 310mg

Exchanges: 2 Starch

Peanut Butter-and-Jelly Sandwich Cookies

Yield: 20 sandwich cookies

¼ cup margarine, softened
¼ cup no-sugar-added creamy peanut butter (such as Fifty-50)
½ cup granulated sugar substitute (such as Splenda)
¼ cup sugar
2 egg whites
1 teaspoon vanilla extract
1¾ cups all-purpose flour
1 teaspoon baking soda
⅛ teaspoon salt
Cooking spray
¾ cup low-sugar strawberry spread

Beat margarine and peanut butter at medium speed of a mixer until creamy. Gradually add sugar substitute and sugar, beating well. Add egg whites and vanilla; beat well. Combine flour, soda, and salt in a small bowl, stirring well. Gradually add flour mixture to creamed mixture, mixing well.

Shape dough into 40 (1-inch) balls. Place balls 2 inches apart on cookie sheets coated with cooking spray. Flatten cookies into 2-inch circles using a flat-bottomed glass. Bake at 350° for 8 minutes or until lightly browned. Cool slightly on cookie sheets; remove from cookie sheets, and let cool completely on wire racks. Spread about 1½ teaspoons strawberry spread on the bottom of half the cooled cookies; top with remaining cookies.

Per Sandwich Cookie:

Calories 97	**Fiber** 0.5g
Fat 4.3g (sat 0.8g)	**Cholesterol** 0mg
Protein 2.5g	**Sodium** 112mg
Carbohydrate 13.3g	**Exchanges:** 1 Starch, 1 Fat

Fudgy Cream Cheese Brownies

Yield: 16 brownies

³⁄₄   cup sugar
¹⁄₄   cup plus 2 tablespoons reduced-calorie stick margarine, softened
1   large egg
1   large egg white
1   tablespoon vanilla extract
¹⁄₂   cup all-purpose flour
¹⁄₄   cup unsweetened cocoa
Cooking spray
1   (8-ounce) block ¹⁄₃-less-fat cream cheese (Neuchâtel), softened
¹⁄₄   cup granulated sugar substitute with aspartame (such as Equal Spoonful)
3   tablespoons 1% low-fat milk

Beat sugar and margarine at medium speed of a mixer until light and fluffy. Add egg, egg white, and vanilla; beat well. Gradually add flour and cocoa, beating well. Pour into an 8-inch square pan coated with cooking spray; set aside.

Beat cream cheese and sugar substitute at high speed of mixer until smooth. Add milk; beat well. Pour cream cheese mixture over chocolate mixture; swirl together using the tip of a knife to create a marbled effect.

Bake at 350° for 30 minutes or until done. Cool completely in pan on a wire rack. Cut into squares.

Per Brownie:

Calories 127	**Fiber** 0.1g
Fat 6.7g (sat 2.8g)	**Cholesterol** 25mg
Protein 2.9g	**Sodium** 107mg
Carbohydrate 14.1g	**Exchanges:** 1 Starch, 1 Fat

(Photograph on cover)

Fish & Shellfish

Orange-Glazed Salmon, page 70

Pecan-Crusted Flounder

Yield: 4 servings

1	slice whole wheat bread, torn
3	tablespoons chopped pecans
1	teaspoon salt-free Creole seasoning
¼	teaspoon salt
4	(4-ounce) flounder fillets
	Butter-flavored cooking spray
2	tablespoons fat-free mayonnaise
½	teaspoon lemon juice

Combine first 4 ingredients in a food processor bowl; process until mixture resembles crumbs. Set aside.

Place fish on a baking sheet coated with cooking spray. Combine mayonnaise and lemon juice. Brush mayonnaise mixture over top of fish. Sprinkle fish evenly with crumb mixture, and coat lightly with cooking spray. Bake at 450° for 15 minutes or until fish flakes easily when tested with a fork. Serve immediately.

Per Serving:

Calories 167	**Fiber** 0.6g
Fat 5.7g (sat 0.7g)	**Cholesterol** 55mg
Protein 22.6g	**Sodium** 371mg
Carbohydrate 6.0g	**Exchanges:** 3 Very Lean Meat, ½ Starch, 1 Fat

If you can't find salt-free Creole seasoning, combine equal amounts of ground red pepper, black pepper, dried oregano, and garlic powder.

Flounder with Curried Papaya Salsa

Yield: 6 servings

1   cup finely chopped papaya (1 medium)
1   cup seeded, finely chopped plum tomato (about 4 medium)
¼   cup finely chopped purple onion
1   tablespoon chopped fresh cilantro or parsley
½   teaspoon peeled, minced ginger
½   teaspoon curry powder
⅛   teaspoon salt
1½   tablespoons lime juice
6   (4-ounce) flounder fillets
Cooking spray

Combine first 8 ingredients in a bowl, stirring well. Cover and chill at least 15 minutes.

Place fish on rack of a broiler pan coated with cooking spray. Broil 5½ inches from heat 6 minutes or until fish flakes easily when tested with a fork. To serve, spoon papaya salsa over fish.

Per Serving:

Calories 141   Fiber 1.7g
Fat 1.8g (sat 0.4g)   Cholesterol 60mg
Protein 22.3g   Sodium 147mg
Carbohydrate 8.9g   Exchanges: ½ Fruit, 3 Very Lean Meat

Seeding a Papaya

Cut the papaya in half vertically with a large, sharp knife.

Scoop out the seeds with a spoon, scraping clean the cavity of each papaya half.

Baked Halibut Provençal

Yield: 2 servings

1   small onion, thinly sliced
1   teaspoon olive oil
½   teaspoon dried rosemary, divided
1   small clove garlic, thinly sliced
1   (1½-inch) piece orange peel
¾   cup canned no-salt-added tomatoes, undrained and chopped
1   teaspoon capers
2   teaspoons fresh orange juice
⅛   teaspoon freshly ground pepper
2   (4-ounce) halibut fillets
2   teaspoons chopped kalamata olives
Fresh herbs (optional)

Combine onion, olive oil, ¼ teaspoon rosemary, garlic, and orange peel in a 13- x 9-inch baking dish. Bake, uncovered, at 400° for 10 minutes or until onion begins to brown, stirring once. Stir in tomatoes and capers; bake 5 additional minutes or until mixture thickens. Stir in orange juice and pepper.

Place halibut on tomato mixture; sprinkle with remaining ¼ teaspoon rosemary. Spoon some of tomato mixture over halibut; bake, uncovered, 10 minutes or until fish flakes easily when tested with a fork. Remove and discard orange peel. Sprinkle with olives. Garnish with fresh herbs, if desired. Serve with roasted potatoes and steamed green beans, if desired (potatoes and beans not included in analysis).

Per Serving:

Calories 194	Fiber 2.0g
Fat 5.4g (sat 0.8g)	Cholesterol 53mg
Protein 32.4g	Sodium 216mg
Carbohydrate 10.6g	Exchanges: 2 Vegetable, 4 Very Lean Meat

Oven-Fried Fish Sticks

Yield: 6 servings

½ (1-ounce) slice white sandwich bread
½ cup yellow cornmeal
1 teaspoon ground pepper
1½ pounds grouper or other white fish fillets
¼ cup fat-free or low-fat buttermilk
Cooking spray
½ teaspoon salt

Tear bread into large pieces, and place in container of a blender; process until crumbly. Spread crumbs on a baking sheet, and bake at 400° for 3 to 5 minutes or until toasted.

Combine breadcrumbs, cornmeal, and pepper in a heavy-duty, zip-top plastic bag; set aside.

Cut fillets diagonally into 1-inch-wide strips. Combine fish strips and buttermilk in a bowl, stirring gently to coat strips. Add buttermilk-coated fish strips to bag; seal bag, and gently turn bag to coat fish strips.

Place fish strips on a baking sheet coated with cooking spray; sprinkle with salt. Bake at 425° for 25 minutes or until fish is crisp and flakes easily when tested with a fork.

Per Serving:

Calories 157	Fiber 1.3g
Fat 1.8g (sat 0.4g)	Cholesterol 42mg
Protein 23.5g	Sodium 289mg
Carbohydrate 10.5g	Exchanges: 1 Starch, 3 Very Lean Meat

Grilled Mahimahi with Pineapple

Yield: 4 servings

3	tablespoons granulated brown sugar substitute
3	tablespoons minced green onions
2	teaspoons peeled, minced ginger
1½	teaspoons minced garlic
½	teaspoon dried crushed red pepper
1½	cups pineapple juice
¼	cup plus 2 tablespoons low-sodium soy sauce
1	tablespoon dark sesame oil
4	(4-ounce) mahimahi fillets
8	(½-inch-thick) fresh pineapple slices

Cooking spray

Combine first 8 ingredients. Place fish and pineapple in a baking dish; add half of juice mixture. Cover and marinate in refrigerator 2 hours, turning occasionally. Divide remaining juice mixture in half; set aside. Remove fish and pineapple from marinade; discard marinade.

Coat grill rack with cooking spray; place on grill over medium-hot coals (350° to 400°). Place fish and pineapple on rack; grill, covered, 5 minutes on each side or until fish flakes easily when tested with a fork, basting frequently with half of reserved juice mixture.

Pour remaining juice mixture through a wire-mesh strainer into a saucepan; discard solids remaining in strainer. Bring to a boil over medium heat. Drizzle over fish and pineapple.

Per Serving:

Calories 231	**Fiber** 2.4g
Fat 3.9g (sat 0.6g)	**Cholesterol** 80mg
Protein 21.1g	**Sodium** 500mg
Carbohydrate 27.4g	**Exchanges:** 2 Fruit, 3 Very Lean Meat

Sunflower Orange Roughy

Yield: 4 servings

¼ cup cornflake crumbs
2 tablespoons dry roasted sunflower kernels
1 teaspoon salt-free seasoning
4 (4-ounce) orange roughy fillets
1 tablespoon lemon juice
Cooking spray

Combine first 3 ingredients in a small bowl. Dip fish in lemon juice, and dredge in crumb mixture.

Place fish on rack of a broiler pan coated with cooking spray. Sprinkle any remaining crumb mixture over fish. Bake at 425° for 10 minutes or until fish flakes easily when tested with a fork. Serve with mixed vegetables and rolls, if desired (vegetables and rolls not included in analysis).

Per Serving:

Calories 201
Fat 9.0g (sat 1.3g)
Protein 23.1g
Carbohydrate 6.0g

Fiber 0.4g
Cholesterol 68mg
Sodium 112mg
Exchanges: ½ Starch, 3 Very Lean Meat, 1 Fat

Orange-Glazed Salmon

Yield: 4 servings

4   (4-ounce) salmon fillets (1 inch thick)
¼   teaspoon salt
¼   teaspoon pepper
Cooking spray
3   tablespoons low-sodium soy sauce
3   tablespoons orange juice
½   teaspoon dark sesame oil

Sprinkle fish with salt and pepper. Coat a large nonstick skillet with cooking spray; place over high heat until hot. Add fish, and cook, uncovered, 3 minutes on each side. Cover and cook 3 additional minutes or until fish flakes easily when tested with a fork. Remove from skillet; set aside, and keep warm.

Add soy sauce and orange juice to skillet; cook over high heat 1 minute, stirring to deglaze skillet. Add oil, and stir well. Pour sauce over fish, and serve immediately.

Per Serving:

Calories 148	**Fiber** 0.1g
Fat 4.6g (sat 0.7g)	**Cholesterol** 59mg
Protein 22.7g	**Sodium** 515mg
Carbohydrate 1.3g	**Exchange:** 3 Lean Meat

(Photograph on page 61)

Citrus- and Pepper-Rubbed Tuna

Yield: 4 servings

2   tablespoons frozen orange juice concentrate, thawed
2   tablespoons salt-free lemon-pepper seasoning
¼   teaspoon salt
4   (4-ounce) tuna steaks
Cooking spray

Combine first 3 ingredients in a small bowl; rub evenly over both sides of fish. Arrange fish on a baking sheet coated with cooking spray.

Bake at 400° for 12 to 14 minutes or until fish flakes easily when tested with a fork.

Per Serving:

Calories 187	**Fiber** 0.9g
Fat 5.8g (sat 1.5g)	**Cholesterol** 43mg
Protein 27.0g	**Sodium** 192mg
Carbohydrate 5.5g	**Exchange:** 4 Very Lean Meat

You can grill the tuna, covered, over medium-hot coals (350° to 400°) 4 to 5 minutes on each side.

Lemon-Pepper Tuna Kabobs

Yield: 4 servings

2	teaspoons grated lemon rind
1	teaspoon ground pepper
½	cup dry white wine
¼	cup fresh lemon juice
2	teaspoons olive oil
1	pound tuna or halibut steaks, cut into 1-inch pieces
2	small yellow squash, cut into 1-inch pieces
1	small sweet red pepper, cut into 1-inch pieces
1	small purple onion, cut into eighths
16	small fresh mushrooms

Cooking spray
Steamed rice (optional)

Combine first 5 ingredients in heavy-duty, zip-top plastic bag; add fish and vegetables. Seal bag; turn bag to coat fish. Marinate in refrigerator 10 minutes.

Remove fish and vegetables from marinade. Place marinade in a small saucepan; bring to a boil. Remove from heat, and set aside. Thread vegetables onto 2 (12-inch) metal skewers. Place on rack of a broiler pan coated with cooking spray. Broil 5½ inches from heat 3 minutes. Thread fish on 2 (12-inch) metal skewers. Add fish kabobs to rack. Broil 6 to 8 minutes or until vegetables are crisp-tender and fish flakes easily when tested with a fork, brushing occasionally with marinade. Remove fish and vegetables from kabobs. Serve with rice, if desired (rice not included in analysis).

Per Serving:

Calories 257	**Fiber** 3.0g
Fat 8.6g (sat 1.8g)	**Cholesterol** 43mg
Protein 29.3g	**Sodium** 52mg
Carbohydrate 12.1g	**Exchanges:** 2 Vegetable, 3 Lean Meat

Maryland Silver Queen Crab Cakes

Yield: 6 servings (serving size: 1 crab cake)

1¼ cups fresh Silver Queen corn cut from the cob (about 2 ears)
1   egg white
1   pound fresh lump crabmeat, drained
¼   cup plus 2 tablespoons fine, dry breadcrumbs
1   tablespoon dried parsley
1   tablespoon low-sodium Worcestershire sauce
1   teaspoon Dijon mustard
¼   teaspoon Old Bay seasoning
Cooking spray

Place corn in food processor bowl; process 8 seconds, scraping sides of processor bowl once. Add egg white; process 2 seconds. Transfer mixture to a bowl; stir in crabmeat and next 5 ingredients. Cover; chill at least 30 minutes.

Shape mixture into 6 patties. Place on a baking sheet coated with cooking spray. Broil 5½ inches from heat 10 minutes on each side or until golden.

Per Serving:

Calories 137	**Fiber** 1.4g
Fat 2.1g (sat 0.3g)	**Cholesterol** 71mg
Protein 16.7g	**Sodium** 316mg
Carbohydrate 13.0g	**Exchanges:** 1 Starch, 2 Very Lean Meat

If Silver Queen corn isn't available, substitute regular white corn.

Linguine and Mussels Marinara

Yield: 4 servings

8	ounces linguine, uncooked
1	pound fresh, farm-raised mussels
2	cups low-fat chunky pasta sauce
¼	teaspoon crushed red pepper flakes
¼	cup chopped fresh basil

Cook pasta according to package directions, omitting salt and fat.

Rinse mussels in cold water; remove beards on mussels, and scrub shells with a brush. Discard opened or cracked mussels. Combine mussels, pasta sauce, and red pepper flakes in a large deep skillet. Cover and bring to a simmer over medium heat; cook 5 minutes or until mussels open. Discard any unopened mussels.

Place ¾ cup drained pasta into each of 4 bowls. Top evenly with mussels and sauce; sprinkle with basil. Serve immediately.

Per Serving:

Calories 187	**Fiber** 3.0g
Fat 2.0g (sat 0.4g)	**Cholesterol** 20mg
Protein 13.2g	**Sodium** 522mg
Carbohydrate 27.9g	**Exchanges:** 2 Starch, 1 Lean Meat

Sweet-and-Sour Shrimp

Yield: 4 servings

1	(8-ounce) can pineapple chunks in juice
1	teaspoon cornstarch
3	tablespoons chili sauce
1	tablespoon low-sodium soy sauce
½	teaspoon garlic powder

Cooking spray

2	teaspoons sesame or vegetable oil
1	medium-size green pepper, coarsely chopped
½	medium onion, sliced
¾	pound peeled and deveined medium-size fresh shrimp

Drain pineapple, reserving juice; set pineapple chunks aside. Combine reserved juice, cornstarch, and next 3 ingredients; set aside.

Coat a large nonstick skillet or wok with cooking spray, and add oil. Place over medium-high heat until hot. Add green pepper and onion; stir-fry 2 to 3 minutes or until crisp-tender. Add shrimp; stir-fry 2 to 3 minutes or until shrimp turn pink.

Stir cornstarch mixture and pineapple chunks into shrimp mixture. Cook over medium heat, stirring constantly, until mixture is thickened and bubbly. Serve over rice, if desired (rice not included in analysis).

Per Serving:

Calories 177	**Fiber** 0.8g
Fat 4.0g (sat 0.7g)	**Cholesterol** 129mg
Protein 18.0g	**Sodium** 397mg
Carbohydrate 16.2g	**Exchanges:** 1 Starch, 2 Lean Meat

Zesty Fettuccine and Shrimp

Yield: 4 servings

8   ounces fettuccine, uncooked
Olive oil-flavored cooking spray
2   teaspoons olive oil
2   teaspoons blackening seasoning
¾   pound peeled and deveined large fresh shrimp
2   tablespoons lemon juice
1   (14½-ounce) can diced tomatoes with roasted garlic, drained
¼   teaspoon pepper

Cook pasta according to package directions, omitting salt and fat.

Coat a large nonstick skillet with cooking spray, and add oil. Place over medium-high heat until hot. Sprinkle blackening seasoning evenly over shrimp. Add shrimp to skillet; cook 2 minutes on each side or until shrimp turn pink. Stir in lemon juice. Add tomatoes and pepper; cook until thoroughly heated.

Spoon shrimp mixture over drained pasta, and serve immediately.

Per Serving:

Calories 344	**Fiber** 1.7g
Fat 4.9g (sat 0.7g)	**Cholesterol** 129mg
Protein 25.2g	**Sodium** 492mg
Carbohydrate 48.2g	**Exchanges:** 3 Starch, 2 Lean Meat

Meatless Main Dishes

Spaghetti Squash with White Bean Provençal, page 94

Vegetable Omelet for One

Yield: 1 serving

¼ cup very thinly sliced carrot
¼ cup very thinly sliced zucchini
3 tablespoons part-skim ricotta cheese
1½ teaspoons chopped fresh or frozen chives
1½ teaspoons chopped fresh dill
½ cup fat-free egg substitute
2 teaspoons water
⅛ teaspoon salt
Cooking spray

Arrange carrot and zucchini is a steamer basket over boiling water. Cover and steam 2 to 3 minutes or until crisp-tender. Drain well. Combine vegetable mixture, ricotta cheese, chives, and dill; set aside.

Combine egg substitute, water, and salt. Coat a 6-inch omelet pan or nonstick skillet with cooking spray; place over medium heat until hot.

Pour egg substitute mixture into skillet. As mixture starts to cook, gently lift edges of omelet with a spatula, and tilt pan so uncooked portion flows underneath. Spoon vegetable mixture over half of omelet. Fold omelet in half; transfer to a serving plate. Serve immediately.

Per Serving:

Calories 150	**Fiber** 1.3g
Fat 4.4g (sat 2.3g)	**Cholesterol** 14mg
Protein 18.1g	**Sodium** 533mg
Carbohydrate 9.0g	**Exchanges:** 1 Vegetable, 2 Very Lean Meat, ½ Fat

Christmas Frittata

Yield: 4 servings

Olive oil-flavored cooking spray
1   tablespoon sliced green onions
2   cloves garlic, minced
1   cup sliced fresh mushrooms
½   cup diced sweet red pepper
¼   cup chopped fresh broccoli flowerets
1½ cups fat-free egg substitute
2   tablespoons grated Parmesan cheese
½   teaspoon dried basil
¼   teaspoon dried oregano
¼   teaspoon pepper
¼   teaspoon salt
⅛   teaspoon dried crushed red pepper
3   tablespoons crumbled feta cheese

Coat a medium-size nonstick skillet with cooking spray; place over medium high heat until hot. Add onions and garlic; sauté 2 minutes. Add mushrooms, sweet red pepper, and broccoli; sauté 3 additional minutes.

Combine egg substitute and next 6 ingredients in a small bowl, stirring well. Pour egg substitute mixture over vegetable mixture. Cover and cook over medium heat 10 minutes or until egg substitute mixture is set. Sprinkle with feta cheese, and serve immediately.

Per Serving:

Calories 89	**Fiber** 0.9g
Fat 2.4g (sat 1.4g)	**Cholesterol** 7mg
Protein 11.9g	**Sodium** 401mg
Carbohydrate 4.9g	**Exchanges:** 1 Vegetable, 1 Lean Meat

Cheddar-Potato Frittata

Yield: 6 servings

1½ cups coarsely chopped round red potato
Cooking spray
1   cup chopped tomato
¼   cup chopped green onions
½   teaspoon pepper
¼   teaspoon salt
1½ cups fat-free egg substitute
½   cup (2 ounces) shredded reduced-fat sharp Cheddar cheese
Green onions (optional)

Cook chopped potato in a saucepan in boiling water to cover 10 to 12 minutes or until tender. Drain well.

Coat a large nonstick skillet with cooking spray; place over medium-high heat until hot. Add potato, tomato, and next 3 ingredients; sauté until onion is tender. Pour egg substitute over vegetable mixture. Cover; cook over medium-low heat 15 minutes or until set. Sprinkle with cheese. Cover; cook 2 minutes or until cheese melts. Cut into 6 wedges, and serve immediately. Garnish with green onions, if desired.

Per Serving:

Calories 100	**Fiber** 1.4g
Fat 2.1g (sat 1.1g)	**Cholesterol** 6mg
Protein 10.1g	**Sodium** 263mg
Carbohydrate 10.5g	**Exchanges:** 1 Starch, 1 Lean Meat

Artichoke Quiche

Yield: 6 servings

2	cups cooked long-grain rice (cooked without salt or fat)
¾	cup (3 ounces) shredded reduced-fat sharp Cheddar cheese, divided
¾	cup fat-free egg substitute, divided
1	teaspoon dried dillweed
½	teaspoon salt
1	small garlic clove, crushed
Cooking spray	
1	(14-ounce) can quartered artichoke hearts, drained
¾	cup fat-free milk
¼	cup sliced green onions
1	tablespoon Dijon mustard
¼	teaspoon ground white pepper
Green onion strips (optional)	

Combine rice, ¼ cup cheese, ¼ cup fat-free egg substitute, dillweed, salt, and garlic; press into a 9-inch pieplate coated with cooking spray. Bake at 350° for 5 minutes.

Arrange artichoke quarters on bottom of rice crust; sprinkle evenly with remaining ½ cup cheese. Combine remaining ½ cup egg substitute, milk, and next 3 ingredients; pour over cheese.

Bake at 350° for 50 minutes or until set. Let stand 5 minutes; cut into wedges. Garnish with green onion strips, if desired.

Per Serving:

Calories 169	**Fiber** 0.4g
Fat 3.5g (sat 1.8g)	**Cholesterol** 11mg
Protein 10.4g	**Sodium** 490mg
Carbohydrate 23.1g	**Exchanges:** 1½ Starch, 1 Lean Meat

Simple Chili Spaghetti

Yield: 6 (1½-cup) servings

8   ounces spaghetti, uncooked
1   (26-ounce) jar fat-free spaghetti sauce
1   (15-ounce) can vegetarian chili
1   (4-ounce) can sliced mushrooms, drained
2   teaspoons chili powder
½   teaspoon garlic powder
Cooking spray
½   cup (2 ounces) reduced-fat shredded sharp Cheddar cheese

Cook pasta according to package directions, omitting salt and fat. Drain.

Combine spaghetti sauce and next 4 ingredients in a medium saucepan. Bring to a boil; cover, reduce heat, and simmer 10 minutes. Coat a 13- x 9-inch baking dish with cooking spray; add spaghetti, and spoon sauce over spaghetti.

Bake at 375° for 25 minutes or until thoroughly heated. Remove from oven, and sprinkle with cheese.

Per Serving:

Calories 272	**Fiber** 8.5g
Fat 2.7g (sat 1.2g)	**Cholesterol** 6mg
Protein 14.4g	**Sodium** 574mg
Carbohydrate 49.2g	**Exchanges:** 3 Starch, 1 Vegetable, 1 Lean Meat

For a make-ahead meal, spoon the spaghetti and the sauce into the dish, cover, and refrigerate. Bake for 35 minutes or until it's thoroughly heated.

Creamy Vegetable Pasta

Yield: 6 (1⅓-cup) servings

8	ounces fettuccine, uncooked
1	pound fresh asparagus
¼	cup water
2	teaspoons margarine
½	teaspoon minced garlic
1	tablespoon all-purpose flour
1¼	cups fat-free milk
3	tablespoons ⅓-less-fat cream cheese
¾	cup shredded fresh Parmesan cheese
1	(15-ounce) can black beans, drained

Cook pasta according to package directions, omitting salt and fat. Drain.

Snap off tough ends of asparagus (Step 1). Remove scales from stalks (Step 2). Cut asparagus into 1-inch pieces; place in a microwave-safe dish. Add ¼ cup water, and cover. Microwave at HIGH 2 minutes; drain.

Melt margarine in a saucepan over medium heat; add garlic. Sauté 1 minute. Add flour; cook, stirring constantly, 1 minute. Add milk, and cook, stirring constantly, 8 minutes or until thickened. Stir in cream cheese; cook, stirring constantly, 2 minutes. Stir in Parmesan cheese. Combine asparagus, cheese sauce, pasta, and beans; toss. Serve warm.

Trimming Asparagus

Step 1

Step 2

Per Serving:

Calories 298	**Fiber** 4.1g
Fat 7.2g (sat 3.5g)	**Cholesterol** 15mg
Protein 16.6g	**Sodium** 419mg
Carbohydrate 42.3g	**Exchanges:** 2 Starch, 2 Vegetable, 1 High-Fat Meat

Baked Ravioli and Vegetables

Yield: 6 servings

10   cups water
1   (9-ounce) package refrigerated light cheese-filled ravioli
1   (16-ounce) package frozen broccoli, cauliflower, and carrots
1   (12-ounce) can fat-free evaporated milk, divided
2   tablespoons all-purpose flour
1   teaspoon dried Italian seasoning
½   teaspoon minced garlic
¼   teaspoon salt
¼   teaspoon ground pepper
¾   cup shredded fresh Parmesan cheese, divided
Cooking spray
2   tablespoons fine, dry breadcrumbs

Bring water to a boil in a Dutch oven. Add pasta and vegetables; cook 5 minutes. Drain.

Combine ½ cup milk and flour; stir well. Combine flour mixture, remaining milk, Italian seasoning, and next 3 ingredients in a saucepan. Cook over medium heat, stirring constantly, until thickened and bubbly. Stir in ½ cup Parmesan cheese.

Combine pasta mixture and cheese sauce; stir. Spoon into an 11- x 7-inch baking dish coated with cooking spray. Sprinkle with breadcrumbs. Bake at 350° for 15 minutes. Sprinkle remaining ¼ cup cheese over breadcrumbs; bake 5 minutes or until lightly browned.

Per Serving:

Calories 262	**Fiber** 3.1g
Fat 6.9g (sat 4.1g)	**Cholesterol** 29mg
Protein 18.2g	**Sodium** 601mg
Carbohydrate 31.7g	**Exchanges:** 2 Starch, 2 Lean Meat

Tortellini with Marinara Sauce

Yield: 6 servings

Cooking spray
1 teaspoon olive oil
¾ cup chopped onion (about 1 small)
1 teaspoon minced garlic
1 (28-ounce) can crushed tomatoes, undrained
2 teaspoons dried Italian seasoning
½ teaspoon sugar
¼ teaspoon salt
2 (9-ounce) packages refrigerated cheese-filled tortellini
¼ cup grated Parmesan cheese

Coat a large saucepan with cooking spray. Add oil, and place over medium-high heat until hot. Add onion and garlic; sauté 4 minutes or until tender. Add tomatoes and next 3 ingredients. Bring to a boil; reduce heat to low, and simmer 20 minutes, stirring occasionally.

Cook pasta according to package directions, omitting salt and fat. Drain.

To serve, place 1 cup pasta on each of 6 plates. Top each serving with ½ cup sauce, and sprinkle evenly with cheese.

Per Serving:

Calories 323	**Fiber** 1.1g
Fat 6.7g (sat 2.9g)	**Cholesterol** 33mg
Protein 17.7g	**Sodium** 676mg
Carbohydrate 48.8g	**Exchanges:** 3 Starch, 1 Vegetable, 1 High-Fat Meat

Pizza Milanese

Yield: 6 servings

1   (9-ounce) package frozen artichoke hearts, thawed and coarsely
         chopped
3   tablespoons fat-free Italian dressing
½   cup part-skim ricotta cheese
⅓   cup crumbled feta cheese
2   tablespoons fat-free sour cream
⅛   teaspoon hot sauce
2   cloves garlic, minced
1   (16-ounce) Italian bread shell (such as Boboli)
2   plum tomatoes, thinly sliced
1   yellow tomato, thinly sliced
⅛   teaspoon paprika
¼   teaspoon cracked pepper

Combine artichokes and Italian dressing; toss gently. Cover and chill 1 hour; drain.

Combine artichokes, ricotta cheese, and next 4 ingredients, stirring well. Spread artichoke mixture evenly over bread shell. Arrange tomato slices over artichoke mixture. Sprinkle with paprika and pepper.

Bake at 450° for 15 to 18 minutes or until thoroughly heated. Cut into 6 wedges; serve warm.

Per Serving:

Calories 272	**Fiber** 1.8g
Fat 6.0g (sat 2.5g)	**Cholesterol** 14mg
Protein 13.2g	**Sodium** 558mg
Carbohydrate 41.2g	**Exchanges:** 2 Starch, 2 Vegetable, 1 Fat

French Bread Pizza

Yield: 6 servings (serving size: 2 portions)

1½ cups pizza-pasta sauce
1   (16-ounce) loaf French bread, cut in half lengthwise
1   (4-ounce) can sliced mushrooms, drained
1   (14-ounce) can artichoke hearts, drained and sliced
4   cloves garlic, sliced
½   cup seeded, chopped tomato
2   tablespoons chopped fresh basil or 2 teaspoons dried basil
½   cup (2 ounces) shredded provolone cheese
½   cup (2 ounces) shredded part-skim mozzarella cheese

Spread pizza sauce evenly over French bread halves.
Arrange mushrooms and next 4 ingredients evenly over sauce.
Sprinkle with cheeses.

Bake at 450° for 10 minutes or until cheese melts and bread is
lightly browned. Cut each bread half into 3 equal portions.

Per Serving:

Calories 345	**Fiber** 3.8g
Fat 5.9g (sat 3.1g)	**Cholesterol** 14mg
Protein 15.0g	**Sodium** 884mg
Carbohydrate 54.3g	**Exchanges:** 3 Starch, 2 Vegetable, 1 Fat

Sesame Broccoli Stir-Fry

Yield: 4 servings

Cooking spray
1   tablespoon dark sesame oil
1   (10½-ounce) package firm low-fat tofu, drained and cubed
4   cups fresh broccoli flowerets
1½ cups diced sweet red pepper
¼   cup low-sodium soy sauce
3   cups cooked instant brown rice (cooked without salt and fat)
1½ tablespoons sesame seeds, toasted

Coat a wok or large nonstick skillet with cooking spray; drizzle oil around top of wok, coating sides. Heat at medium-high (375°) until hot. Add tofu; stir-fry 5 to 6 minutes or until tofu starts to brown. Remove tofu from wok; set aside, and keep warm.

Add broccoli, red pepper, and soy sauce to wok; stir-fry 3 minutes or until vegetables are crisp-tender. Add tofu, and stir-fry 30 seconds or until thoroughly heated. To serve, spoon ¾ cup rice onto each plate. Top evenly with broccoli mixture. Sprinkle evenly with sesame seeds.

Per Serving:

Calories 302	**Fiber** 6.6g
Fat 9.6g (sat 0.9g)	**Cholesterol** 0mg
Protein 21.4g	**Sodium** 484mg
Carbohydrate 42.1g	**Exchanges:** 2 Starch, 2 Vegetable, 2 Lean Meat, ½ Fat

Think of tofu as the "cheese" that's made from soy milk. Tofu is a good source of nonmeat protein and is high in calcium, iron, vitamin B, and vitamin E.

Soy products like tofu may also help increase bone density and minimize symptoms of menopause.

Spaghetti Squash with White Bean Provençal

Yield: 4 servings

1   (2½-pound) spaghetti squash
Cooking spray
1   teaspoon roasted garlic-flavored vegetable oil
2   cups thinly sliced leek (about 1 leek)
2   (16-ounce) cans navy beans, drained
1   (14½-ounce) can no-salt-added stewed tomatoes, undrained
2   tablespoons chopped ripe olives
1   tablespoon balsamic vinegar
¼   teaspoon salt
¼   teaspoon pepper

Wash squash; cut in half lengthwise. Remove and discard seeds. Place squash, cut sides down, in a 13- x 9-inch baking dish coated with cooking spray. Bake at 350° for 45 minutes or until tender; let cool slightly. Using a fork, remove spaghetti-like strands from squash; discard shells. Set strands aside, and keep warm.

Coat a saucepan with cooking spray; add oil. Place over medium-high heat until hot. Add leek; sauté 3 minutes. Add beans and tomato; cook over medium heat 5 minutes. Stir in olives and next 3 ingredients; cook until thoroughly heated. Spoon mixture over squash.

Per Serving:

Calories 226	**Fiber** 6.8g
Fat 2.9g (sat 0.6g)	**Cholesterol** 0mg
Protein 10.5g	**Sodium** 508mg
Carbohydrate 43.0g	**Exchanges:** 2 Starch, 2 Vegetable, ½ Fat

(Photograph on page 79)

Meats

Roasted Lamb and Vegetables, page 109

Ground Beef Stroganoff

Yield: 5 servings

8	ounces wide egg noodles, uncooked
1	pound ground round
3	green onions, sliced, or 1 cup chopped onion
1	(8-ounce) package sliced fresh mushrooms
1	(12-ounce) jar fat-free beef gravy
1	(8-ounce) carton fat-free sour cream
¼	teaspoon garlic salt
¼	teaspoon freshly ground pepper
1	tablespoon dry sherry (optional)

Prepare noodles according to package directions, omitting salt and fat. Drain.

Cook meat, green onions, and mushrooms in a large nonstick skillet until meat is browned, stirring until it crumbles; drain.

Return meat mixture to skillet; add gravy and next 3 ingredients, stirring well. Cook over medium heat 3 to 5 minutes or until thoroughly heated. Stir in sherry, if desired. To serve, spoon beef mixture evenly over ¾-cup portions of noodles.

Per Serving:

Calories 367	**Fiber** 3.9g
Fat 7.6g (sat 2.4g)	**Cholesterol** 98mg
Protein 31.1g	**Sodium** 611mg
Carbohydrate 42.9g	**Exchanges:** 3 Starch, 3 Lean Meat

Cheeseburger Meat Loaves

Yield: 4 servings

¾ pound ground round
1 cup crushed fat-free saltine crackers
¾ cup finely chopped onion (about 1 small)
½ cup finely chopped green pepper (about 1 small)
1 tablespoon low-sodium Worcestershire sauce
2 egg whites, lightly beaten
½ teaspoon minced garlic (about 1 clove)
2 (¾-ounce) slices fat-free American cheese, quartered
Cooking spray
3 tablespoons reduced-calorie ketchup

Combine first 7 ingredients in a large bowl; mix well. Divide meat mixture into 4 equal portions. Shape each portion around 2 pieces of cheese, forming a small loaf.

Place loaves in a shallow pan coated with cooking spray. Brush loaves evenly with ketchup. Bake at 350° for 30 minutes or until done. Let stand 10 minutes before serving.

Per Serving:

Calories 220	**Fiber** 0.8g
Fat 4.5g (sat 1.5g)	**Cholesterol** 51mg
Protein 25.2g	**Sodium** 404mg
Carbohydrate 17.5g	**Exchanges:** 1 Starch, 3 Lean Meat

Quick-and-Easy Salisbury Steaks

Yield: 4 servings

1	pound ground round
¼	teaspoon garlic powder
¼	teaspoon salt
¼	teaspoon ground pepper
Cooking spray	
1	(8-ounce) package presliced fresh mushrooms
¼	cup chopped onion
1	tablespoon finely chopped fresh thyme or 1 teaspoon dried thyme
2	tablespoons dry sherry or white wine
1	(12-ounce) jar fat-free beef gravy
Fresh thyme sprigs (optional)	

Combine first 4 ingredients in a medium bowl; mix well. Shape mixture into 4 (½-inch-thick) patties.

Coat a large nonstick skillet with cooking spray; place over medium heat until hot. Add patties, and cook 4 to 5 minutes on each side or until done. Remove patties from skillet, and set aside.

Increase heat to medium-high; add mushrooms, onion, and thyme; sauté 3 minutes or until vegetables are tender. Add sherry; cook 1 minute. Stir in gravy; return patties to skillet. Cook 2 minutes or until thoroughly heated. Garnish with thyme, if desired.

Per Serving:

Calories 208	Fiber 1.0g
Fat 7.2g (sat 2.5g)	Cholesterol 70mg
Protein 27.1g	Sodium 729mg
Carbohydrate 8.5g	Exchanges: ½ Starch, 4 Lean Meat

Flank Steak with Mushrooms

Yield: 4 servings

¼ cup low-sodium soy sauce
2 tablespoons lemon juice
1 teaspoon freeze-dried chives
¼ teaspoon dried marjoram
2 cloves garlic, minced
1 (1-pound) lean flank steak, trimmed
Cooking spray
1 teaspoon olive oil
3 cups sliced fresh mushrooms
2 tablespoons minced fresh parsley

Combine first 5 ingredients in a heavy-duty, zip-top plastic bag. Add steak; seal bag, and shake until well coated. Marinate in refrigerator 8 hours, turning occasionally.

Remove steak from marinade, reserving marinade. Slice steak diagonally across grain into ¼-inch-wide strips. Coat a large non-stick skillet with cooking spray; add oil. Place over medium-high heat until hot. Add steak; cook 5 minutes or until browned on all sides, stirring frequently. Remove steak from skillet. Drain and pat dry. Wipe drippings from skillet.

Coat skillet with cooking spray, and place over medium-high heat until hot. Add mushrooms; sauté 3 minutes. Stir in reserved marinade and parsley. Cover, reduce heat to medium, and cook 5 minutes. Return steak to skillet; cook until thoroughly heated.

Per Serving:

Calories 248
Fat 14.5g (sat 5.6g)
Protein 23.3g
Carbohydrate 4.6g

Fiber 1.0g
Cholesterol 60mg
Sodium 464mg
Exchanges: 1 Vegetable, 3 Medium-Fat Meat

Beef Stir-Fry with Oyster Sauce

Yield: 4 servings

1	large bag boil-in-bag rice
1	pound boneless top sirloin
Cooking spray	
1	teaspoon minced garlic
1	(16-ounce) package frozen broccoli stir-fry vegetables, thawed
¼	cup oyster sauce or Worcestershire sauce

Prepare rice according to package directions, omitting salt and fat, to make 3 cups cooked rice.

Slice meat across grain into very thin strips. Coat a wok or large nonstick skillet with cooking spray; heat at medium-high (375°) until hot. Add meat and garlic; stir-fry until browned.

Add broccoli stir-fry vegetables and oyster sauce to skillet; stir-fry 5 minutes or until thoroughly heated. To serve, spoon beef mixture evenly over ¾-cup portions of rice.

Per Serving:

Calories 366	**Fiber** 3.4g
Fat 6.0g (sat 2.1g)	**Cholesterol** 69mg
Protein 29.6g	**Sodium** 345mg
Carbohydrate 47.9g	**Exchanges:** 3 Starch, 1 Vegetable, 3 Lean Meat

Slow-Cooked Beef Burgundy

Yield: 8 servings

¼ cup all-purpose flour
½ teaspoon salt
½ teaspoon ground pepper
2 pounds lean, boneless round steak, cut into 1½-inch pieces
1 teaspoon minced garlic
¾ cup dry red wine
¾ cup canned no-salt-added beef broth
1 tablespoon tomato paste
1 tablespoon chopped fresh thyme or 1 teaspoon dried thyme
8 ounces baby carrots (about 40 small)
1 large onion, cut into eighths
1 bay leaf
1 (8-ounce) package sliced fresh mushrooms
4 cups hot cooked yolk-free medium egg noodles
   (cooked without salt or fat)

Combine first 3 ingredients in a heavy-duty, zip-top plastic bag; add beef, and seal bag. Shake to coat. Place a large nonstick skillet over medium-high heat until hot. Add garlic and beef; cook 10 minutes or until browned on all sides, stirring often.

Transfer beef to a 4-quart electric slow cooker. Add wine and next 6 ingredients. Cover and cook on high setting 6 hours. Or cover and cook on high setting 1 hour; reduce to low setting, and cook 7 hours. Add mushrooms 1 hour before cooking is completed. Discard bay leaf. Stir. Spoon beef mixture evenly over ½-cup portions of noodles.

Per Serving:

Calories 299	Fiber 2.6g
Fat 5.3g (sat 1.7g)	Cholesterol 65mg
Protein 30.8g	Sodium 232mg
Carbohydrate 26.7g	Exchanges: 2 Starch, 3 Lean Meat

Filet Mignon with Béarnaise Sauce

Yield: 4 servings

3	tablespoons dry white wine
2	tablespoons tarragon vinegar
1	tablespoon minced shallots
½	teaspoon dried tarragon
¼	teaspoon freshly ground pepper
¼	cup fat-free egg substitute
3	tablespoons reduced-calorie margarine
1	tablespoon fat-free sour cream
4	(4-ounce) beef tenderloin steaks
Cooking spray	
½	teaspoon salt-free lemon-pepper seasoning

Combine first 5 ingredients in a skillet. Bring to a boil. Reduce heat, and simmer, uncovered, until reduced to 2 tablespoons.

Pour mixture through a strainer into the top of a double boiler; discard shallots. Add egg substitute; stir well. Bring water to a boil, stirring constantly. Reduce heat to low. Add margarine, 1 tablespoon at a time, stirring constantly with a wire whisk until blended. Cook, stirring constantly, until slightly thickened. Remove from heat; stir in sour cream. Set aside; keep warm.

Place steaks on rack of a broiler pan coated with cooking spray. Sprinkle with seasoning. Broil 5½ inches from heat 8 minutes on each side or to desired degree of doneness. Serve with sauce.

Per Serving:

Calories 232	**Fiber** 0.1g
Fat 13.5g (sat 3.1g)	**Cholesterol** 71mg
Protein 25.9g	**Sodium** 162mg
Carbohydrate 1.0g	**Exchanges:** 3 Medium-Fat Meat

Veal in Lime Cream Sauce

Yield: 4 servings

1   pound veal cutlets (¼ inch thick)
¼   teaspoon salt
¼   teaspoon freshly ground pepper
Butter-flavored cooking spray
2   tablespoons fresh lime juice
2   tablespoons dry white wine
1   tablespoon plus 1 teaspoon all-purpose flour
½   cup low-sodium chicken broth
⅔   cup fat-free evaporated milk
½   teaspoon lime zest

Sprinkle veal with salt and pepper. Coat a large nonstick skillet with cooking spray; place over medium-high heat until hot. Add cutlets, and cook 1 minute on each side or until browned. Remove from skillet; set aside, and keep warm.

Add lime juice and wine to skillet; cook over high heat 1 minute or until mixture is reduced by half. Combine flour, broth, and milk; stir well. Add to lime juice mixture. Cook over medium heat, stirring constantly, 5 minutes or until thickened and bubbly. Return veal to skillet; cook until thoroughly heated. Transfer to a serving platter. Sprinkle with lime zest, and serve immediately.

Per Serving:

Calories 218	**Fiber** 0.1g
Fat 6.1g (sat 1.6g)	**Cholesterol** 102mg
Protein 31.0g	**Sodium** 282mg
Carbohydrate 8.1g	**Exchanges:** ½ Starch, 4 Very Lean Meat

Osso Buco

Yield: 4 servings

4   (5-ounce) veal shanks
2   tablespoons all-purpose flour
Olive oil-flavored cooking spray
½   cup chopped onion
½   cup chopped carrot
2   (14½-ounce) cans no-salt-added diced tomatoes, undrained
½   cup dry white wine
½   cup canned no-salt-added beef broth
½   teaspoon salt
¼   teaspoon freshly ground pepper
1½   teaspoons minced fresh parsley (optional)
1½   teaspoons grated lemon rind (optional)
1½   teaspoons minced garlic (optional)

Trim fat from veal; dredge in flour. Coat a large Dutch oven with cooking spray; place over medium-high heat until hot. Add veal; cook until browned on all sides. Remove veal; set aside, and keep warm. Wipe drippings from Dutch oven.

Coat Dutch oven with cooking spray; place over medium-high heat until hot. Add onion and carrot; sauté until tender. Stir in tomato and next 4 ingredients; add veal. Bring to a boil; cover, reduce heat, and simmer 20 minutes. Uncover and simmer 30 minutes or until veal is tender. Spoon vegetable mixture over veal. If desired, sprinkle with parsley, lemon rind, and garlic.

Per Serving:

Calories 220
Fat 3.8g (sat 1.0g)
Protein 25.6g
Carbohydrate 20.4g

Fiber 2.4g
Cholesterol 98mg
Sodium 443mg
Exchanges: 1 Starch, 1 Vegetable, 3 Very Lean Meat

Veal Parmesan with Tomato Salsa

Yield: 4 servings

4   (6-ounce) lean veal loin chops (¾ inch thick)
½   cup crushed toasted whole grain wheat flake cereal
⅛   cup grated Parmesan cheese
1   egg white, lightly beaten
Cooking spray
¼   cup (1 ounce) shredded part-skim mozzarella cheese
1   cup chunky salsa with vegetables

Trim fat from veal. Combine cereal and Parmesan cheese in a shallow bowl. Dip veal in egg white, and dredge in cereal mixture. Place veal in a 13- x 9-inch baking dish coated with cooking spray. Cover and chill 30 minutes.

Bake veal, uncovered, at 375° for 30 to 35 minutes or until tender. Sprinkle with mozzarella cheese; bake 5 additional minutes or until cheese melts. To serve, spoon salsa evenly over veal.

Per Serving:

Calories 200	**Fiber** 1.6g
Fat 6.0g (sat 2.4g)	**Cholesterol** 97mg
Protein 27.6g	**Sodium** 399mg
Carbohydrate 8.2g	**Exchanges:** ½ Starch, 4 Very Lean Meat

Roasted Lamb and Vegetables

Yield: 14 servings

1 (3½-pound) lean boneless leg of lamb, trimmed
7 large cloves garlic, sliced
2 tablespoons chopped fresh rosemary
1 teaspoon salt
1 teaspoon freshly ground pepper
2¾ pounds small round red potatoes
2 (1-pound) packages baby carrots
1 (14¼-ounce) can no-salt-added beef broth
¼ cup water
2 tablespoons cornstarch

Make ¼-inch-deep slits in lamb; insert garlic slices. Combine rosemary, salt, and pepper; sprinkle half of mixture over lamb. Insert meat thermometer into thickest part of lamb. Place in a large roasting pan; add potatoes, carrots, and broth. Sprinkle vegetables with remaining rosemary mixture. Bake, uncovered, at 350° for 2 hours or until meat thermometer registers 145°, stirring vegetables occasionally.

Transfer lamb and vegetables to a platter; keep warm. Skim fat from pan juices. Combine water and cornstarch; stir until smooth. Add to pan juices, stirring with a wire whisk. Bring to a boil over medium heat, stirring constantly. Cook, stirring constantly, until thickened. Serve gravy with lamb and vegetables.

Per Serving:

Calories 267	**Fiber** 3.8g
Fat 6.9g (sat 2.4g)	**Cholesterol** 76mg
Protein 26.9g	**Sodium** 256mg
Carbohydrate 23.3g	**Exchanges:** 1 Starch, 2 Vegetable, 3 Lean Meat

(Photograph on page 95)

Lamb Chops with Minted Sour Cream Sauce

Yield: 2 servings
(serving size: 2 lamb chops and 2 tablespoons sauce)

¼ cup fat-free sour cream
⅛ teaspoon salt
½ teaspoon dried mint leaves
4 (4-ounce) lean lamb loin chops (1 inch thick)
¼ teaspoon salt
⅛ teaspoon black pepper
⅛ teaspoon garlic powder
Cooking spray

Combine first 3 ingredients; stir well, and set aside.

Trim fat from lamb; sprinkle lamb evenly with ¼ teaspoon salt, pepper, and garlic powder.

Coat a large nonstick skillet with cooking spray; place over medium-high heat until hot. Add lamb. Cook 3 to 4 minutes on each side or until browned. Reduce heat to medium-low; cook 2 to 3 additional minutes on each side or to desired degree of doneness. Serve with sour cream sauce.

Per Serving:

Calories 267

Fat 11.3g (sat 4.0g)

Protein 36.0g

Carbohydrate 2.0g

Fiber 0.0g

Cholesterol 108mg

Sodium 549mg

Exchanges: 5 Lean Meat

The nearer the bone, the sweeter the meat.

British proverb

Speedy Pork Tostadas

Yield: 4 servings

4   (8-inch) fat-free flour tortillas
Cooking spray
½   pound pork tenderloin, cut into short, thin strips
1   teaspoon minced garlic
1   teaspoon ground cumin
1   (16-ounce) can pinto beans, drained
½   cup chunky salsa
2   cups shredded romaine lettuce
½   cup (2 ounces) shredded reduced-fat Cheddar cheese
1   cup chopped tomato (about 1 medium)
¼   cup fat-free sour cream

Arrange tortillas on a baking sheet; coat both sides lightly with cooking spray. Bake at 375° for 7 to 8 minutes or until golden.

Coat a large nonstick skillet with cooking spray; place over medium-high heat until hot. Add pork, garlic, and cumin; cook 3 minutes or until pork is browned on all sides, stirring frequently. Add beans and salsa; cook 4 minutes or until pork is tender.

To serve, place tortillas on 4 plates; arrange lettuce evenly over tortillas. Top evenly with pork mixture, cheese, tomato, and sour cream.

Per Serving:

Calories 339

Fat 8.2g (sat 2.6g)

Protein 25.1g

Carbohydrate 40.6g

Fiber 5.8g

Cholesterol 46mg

Sodium 577mg

Exchanges: 2 Starch, 2 Vegetable, 2 Lean Meat

Skillet Chops and Rice

Yield: 4 servings

4   (6-ounce) center-cut pork chops ($\frac{1}{2}$ inch thick)
Cooking spray
1$\frac{1}{2}$ cups quick-cooking 5-minute rice, uncooked
$\frac{2}{3}$ cup water
$\frac{1}{2}$ cup chopped onion
$\frac{1}{4}$ teaspoon pepper
1   (14$\frac{1}{2}$-ounce) can Italian-style stewed tomatoes, undrained and chopped
1   (8-ounce) can no-salt-added tomato sauce

Trim fat from pork. Coat a large nonstick skillet with cooking spray, and place over medium-high heat until hot. Add pork, and cook 2 minutes on each side. Remove from skillet; set aside.

Combine rice and remaining 5 ingredients in skillet; bring to a boil. Arrange pork over rice mixture. Cover, reduce heat, and cook 5 minutes or until liquid is absorbed and rice is done.

Per Serving:

Calories 375	**Fiber** 2.2g
Fat 8.5g (sat 2.9g)	**Cholesterol** 71mg
Protein 29.5g	**Sodium** 352mg
Carbohydrate 42.9g	**Exchanges:** 2 Starch, 2 Vegetable, 3 Lean Meat

Avoid fried meats which angry up the blood.

LEROY "SATCHEL" PAGE, Baseball Player,
How To Stay Young

Pork and Sauerkraut Casserole

Yield: 6 servings

Cooking spray
6   (4-ounce) boneless center-cut pork loin chops
1   teaspoon vegetable oil
1   cup chopped onion
½   cup thinly sliced carrot
2   cups sauerkraut
½   cup dry white wine
½   cup low-sodium chicken broth
1   teaspoon freshly ground pepper
¼   cup chopped fresh parsley

Coat a large nonstick skillet with cooking spray; place over medium-high heat until hot. Add pork, and cook 6 minutes on each side or until browned. Remove pork from skillet. Drain and pat dry with paper towels. Wipe drippings from skillet with paper towel.

Coat skillet with cooking spray; add oil. Place over medium-high heat until hot. Add onion and carrot; sauté 4 minutes or until tender. Add sauerkraut and next 3 ingredients; cook over medium heat 8 minutes. Place sauerkraut mixture in a 13- x 9-inch baking dish coated with cooking spray. Arrange pork over sauerkraut mixture. Cover and bake at 350° for 1 hour and 15 minutes or until pork is tender. Sprinkle with parsley.

Per Serving:

Calories 215

Fat 10.0g (sat 2.9g)

Protein 26.5g

Carbohydrate 5.1g

Fiber 2.1g

Cholesterol 71mg

Sodium 422mg

Exchanges: 1 Vegetable, 3½ Lean Meat

Ham and Hash Brown Casserole

Yield: 8 (1¼-cup) servings

3   tablespoons all-purpose flour
1¾ cups fat-free evaporated milk, divided
¾   teaspoon dry mustard
¼   teaspoon pepper
⅛   teaspoon salt
4   ounces reduced-fat loaf process cheese spread (such as Velveeta Light), cubed
1   (8-ounce) carton fat-free sour cream
8   ounces reduced-fat, low-salt ham, chopped (about 2 cups)
1   (32-ounce) package frozen cubed hash browns with onions, thawed
Cooking spray

Combine flour and ½ cup milk, stirring until smooth. Combine flour mixture, remaining 1¼ cups milk, mustard, pepper, and salt in a medium saucepan, stirring well. Cook over medium heat, stirring constantly, until milk mixture is thickened and bubbly. Remove from heat; add cheese, stirring until cheese melts. Stir in sour cream.

Combine cheese mixture, ham, and hash browns in a large bowl, stirring well. Spoon potato mixture into a 13- x 9-inch baking dish coated with cooking spray. Cover and bake at 350° for 30 minutes. Uncover and bake 30 to 35 additional minutes or until golden.

Per Serving:

Calories 201	**Fiber** 2.1g
Fat 3.2g (sat 1.5g)	**Cholesterol** 21mg
Protein 15.7g	**Sodium** 570mg
Carbohydrate 27.8g	**Exchanges:** 2 Starch, 1 Lean Meat

Poultry

Chicken with Mushroom Sauce, page 134

Speedy Herbed Chicken Hash

Yield: 5 servings (serving size: about 1⅓ cups)

Cooking spray
2   teaspoons margarine
1   (26-ounce) package frozen country-style hash brown potatoes, thawed
1   (10-ounce) package chopped pepper, onion, and celery blend, thawed
2½ cups chopped cooked chicken breast
½   cup fat-free, reduced-sodium chicken broth
½   teaspoon ground sage
½   teaspoon dried rosemary, crushed
¼   teaspoon salt
¼   teaspoon ground pepper

Coat a large nonstick skillet with cooking spray; add margarine. Place over medium-high heat until margarine melts. Add potatoes and vegetable blend; cook 7 minutes or until potatoes begin to brown, stirring occasionally.

Add chicken and remaining ingredients; stir well. Cover and cook over medium-high heat 5 minutes or until thoroughly heated.

Per Serving:

Calories 290	**Fiber** 1.6g
Fat 7.6g (sat 1.9g)	**Cholesterol** 69mg
Protein 24.8g	**Sodium** 216mg
Carbohydrate 29.4g	**Exchanges:** 3 Lean Meat, 2 Starch

If you can't find the frozen vegetable blend, use 5 ounces of frozen chopped onion and 5 ounces of frozen chopped pepper.

Smoked Chicken-Tomato Pasta

Yield: 6 (1-cup) servings

2   (10½-ounce) cans low-sodium chicken broth
2   cups water
6   ounces penne pasta, uncooked
¾   cup coarsely chopped dried tomatoes
Olive oil-flavored cooking spray
1   cup chopped green pepper
½   cup chopped onion
1   clove garlic, minced
1   tablespoon margarine
1½   tablespoons all-purpose flour
1   cup fat-free milk
8   ounces smoked chicken breast, cubed
2   tablespoons chopped fresh basil
⅓   cup grated Parmesan cheese

Bring broth and 2 cups water to a boil in a large saucepan. Add pasta and tomatoes; cook 10 minutes or until pasta is tender. Drain.

Coat a skillet with cooking spray; place over medium-high heat until hot. Add pepper, onion, and garlic; sauté until tender. Set aside; keep warm. Melt margarine in a large saucepan over low heat. Add flour; cook, stirring constantly, 1 minute. Add milk, stirring constantly. Cook, stirring constantly, until thickened. Stir in pasta, pepper mixture, chicken, and basil. Cook until thoroughly heated. Sprinkle with cheese.

Per Serving:

Calories 244
Fat 5.9g (sat 1.9g)
Protein 16.1g
Carbohydrate 32.6g

Fiber 1.4g
Cholesterol 22mg
Sodium 766mg
Exchanges: 2 Starch, 1 Vegetable, 1 Very Lean Meat, ½ Fat

Black Bean and Chicken Pizzas

Yield: 4 servings

2	cups shredded cooked chicken
1	teaspoon ground cumin
1	cup chunky salsa
4	(6-inch) Italian bread shells (such as Boboli)
1	(15-ounce) can no-salt-added black beans, rinsed and drained
¾	cup (3 ounces) shredded reduced-fat sharp Cheddar cheese
½	cup thinly sliced green onions (about 2 large)

Sprinkle chicken with cumin; toss well.

Spread salsa evenly over bread shells to within ½ inch of edges; arrange chicken over salsa. Layer beans over chicken; sprinkle with cheese. Place pizzas on a large ungreased baking sheet.

Bake at 450° for 10 minutes or until cheese melts. Sprinkle with green onions. Serve immediately.

Per Serving:

Calories 437	Fiber 4.1g
Fat 10.3g (sat 4.2g)	Cholesterol 80mg
Protein 42.6g	Sodium 806mg
Carbohydrate 41.9g	Exchanges: 3 Starch, 4 Lean Meat

Sesame Chicken Tenders

Yield: 4 servings

2	egg whites, lightly beaten
2	tablespoons low-sodium soy sauce
1	tablespoon honey
¾	cup crushed cornflakes cereal
1½	tablespoons sesame seeds
½	teaspoon paprika
¼	teaspoon salt
¼	teaspoon ground pepper
1	pound chicken tenders

Cooking spray
Fat-free Ranch dressing (optional)
Spicy mustard (optional)
Barbecue sauce (optional)

Combine first 3 ingredients in a medium bowl, stirring with a wire whisk. Combine next 5 ingredients in a small bowl.

Dip chicken in egg white mixture, and dredge in cereal mixture. Place chicken on a baking sheet coated with cooking spray. Bake at 400° for 23 to 25 minutes or until crispy and golden. Serve with fat-free Ranch dressing, spicy mustard, or barbecue sauce, if desired (condiments not included in analysis).

Per Serving:

Calories 239	**Fiber** 0.4g
Fat 3.3g (sat 0.6g)	**Cholesterol** 66mg
Protein 29.7g	**Sodium** 609mg
Carbohydrate 20.4g	**Exchanges:** 1½ Starch, 3½ Very Lean Meat

Sweet Curry Chicken

Yield: 6 servings

1	(20-ounce) can unsweetened pineapple tidbits
¼	cup unsweetened pineapple juice
1	tablespoon cornstarch
1¾	teaspoons curry powder
½	teaspoon salt
2	teaspoons honey
3	tablespoons all-purpose flour
½	teaspoon dried crushed red pepper
1½	pounds unbreaded chicken breast nuggets
1	tablespoon vegetable oil
1	green pepper, seeded and cut into thin strips
1	sweet yellow pepper, seeded and cut into thin strips

Drain pineapple, reserving juice. Set pineapple aside. Combine reserved juice, ¼ cup juice, and next 4 ingredients; set aside.

Place flour and red pepper in a heavy-duty, zip-top plastic bag. Add chicken, and seal bag; shake until chicken is lightly coated. Shake off excess flour.

Heat oil in a skillet over medium-high heat. Add chicken; cook 4 minutes on each side. Remove chicken. Add pepper strips to skillet; sauté 2 minutes or until crisp-tender. Add chicken, pineapple, and pineapple juice mixture. Bring to a boil over medium heat, stirring constantly. Reduce heat; simmer 3 minutes or until thickened and bubbly.

Per Serving:

Calories 227	Fiber 1.8g
Fat 4.1g (sat 0.7g)	Cholesterol 47mg
Protein 19.8g	Sodium 253mg
Carbohydrate 27.4g	Exchanges: 1 Starch, 1 Fruit, 3 Very Lean Meat

Gingered Chicken Stir-Fry

Yield: 4 servings

1   regular-size bag boil-in-bag rice, uncooked
⅓   cup stir-fry sauce
½   teaspoon ground ginger
½   teaspoon garlic powder
Cooking spray
2   teaspoons dark sesame oil
1   pound skinned, boned chicken breast halves, cut into bite-size pieces
1   (16-ounce) package frozen Oriental-style vegetables

Cook rice according to package directions, omitting salt and fat.

Combine stir-fry sauce, ginger, and garlic powder in a small bowl, stirring well; set aside.

Coat a large nonstick skillet with cooking spray; add oil, and place over medium-high heat until hot. Add chicken, and stir-fry 4 minutes or until chicken is done. Remove from skillet; set aside.

Add vegetables to skillet; stir-fry 3 minutes. Stir in chicken and stir-fry sauce mixture. Cook over medium-high heat until thoroughly heated. To serve, spoon chicken mixture evenly over ½-cup portions of rice.

Per Serving:

Calories 315	**Fiber** 2.5g
Fat 4.0g (sat 0.7g)	**Cholesterol** 66mg
Protein 31.3g	**Sodium** 796mg
Carbohydrate 37.4g	**Exchanges:** 2 Starch, 1 Vegetable, 3 Very Lean Meat

One regular-size bag of boil-in-bag rice makes 2 cups of cooked rice.

Moroccan Chicken with Couscous

Yield: 4 servings

1	pound skinned, boned chicken breast halves
½	teaspoon ground ginger
¼	teaspoon ground cumin
¼	teaspoon ground turmeric
¼	teaspoon salt
Cooking spray	
1	teaspoon vegetable oil
½	teaspoon minced garlic
1	(16-ounce) can fat-free, reduced-sodium chicken broth
1	cup frozen English peas, thawed
1	cup couscous, uncooked
¼	cup chopped fresh cilantro or parsley

Cut chicken lengthwise into 1-inch-wide strips. Combine ginger and next 3 ingredients. Sprinkle evenly over chicken; set aside.

Coat a large nonstick skillet with cooking spray; add oil, and place over medium-high heat until hot. Add chicken and garlic; sauté 3 minutes or until chicken is lightly browned. Add broth and peas; bring to a boil. Reduce heat, and simmer 2 minutes or until chicken is done. Stir in couscous; cover and remove from heat. Let stand 5 minutes or until liquid is absorbed. Sprinkle with cilantro.

Per Serving:

Calories 329	**Fiber** 3.3g
Fat 3.3g (sat 0.6g)	**Cholesterol** 66mg
Protein 34.0g	**Sodium** 506mg
Carbohydrate 38.3g	**Exchanges:** 2 Starch, 1 Vegetable, 4 Very Lean Meat

Chicken in Tomato-Vegetable Sauce

Yield: 4 servings

1   tablespoon olive oil
1   cup sliced leek (about 1 large)
2   cloves garlic, minced
4   (4-ounce) skinned, boned chicken breast halves, cut into thin strips
2   teaspoons dried Italian seasoning
1   (14½-ounce) can no-salt-added diced tomatoes, undrained
1   medium zucchini, sliced
½   cup low-sodium chicken broth
¼   cup dry white wine
¼   teaspoon salt
¼   cup no-salt-added tomato paste
2   cups cooked long-grain rice (cooked without salt or fat)
2   tablespoons freshly grated Parmesan cheese
Fresh basil sprigs (optional)

Heat oil in a large nonstick skillet over medium-high heat. Add leek and garlic; sauté 3 minutes or until tender. Add chicken, and sauté 7 minutes or until chicken is done. Stir in seasoning. Remove chicken from skillet; set aside, and keep warm.

Add tomato and next 4 ingredients to skillet; bring to a boil. Stir in tomato paste; cover, reduce heat, and simmer 10 minutes. Add chicken; cook until thoroughly heated. Spoon chicken mixture evenly over ½-cup portions of rice. Sprinkle evenly with Parmesan cheese. Garnish with basil sprigs, if desired.

Per Serving:

Calories 326	Fiber 2.2g
Fat 6.5g (sat 1.5g)	Cholesterol 68mg
Protein 31.7g	Sodium 301mg
Carbohydrate 34.3g	Exchanges: 2 Starch, 1 Vegetable, 3 Lean Meat

Crispy Cornmeal Chicken

Yield: 4 servings
(serving size: 1 chicken breast half and 2 tablespoons salsa)

4	(4-ounce) skinned, boned chicken breast halves
⅓	cup yellow cornmeal
1	teaspoon chili powder
¼	teaspoon garlic powder
¼	teaspoon salt
1	tablespoon all-purpose flour
2	large egg whites, lightly beaten
2	teaspoons vegetable oil
½	cup salsa

Place chicken between 2 sheets of heavy-duty plastic wrap, and flatten to ½-inch thickness, using a meat mallet or rolling pin.

Combine cornmeal and next 3 ingredients in a small bowl. Sprinkle flour evenly over each chicken breast half; dip in egg whites, and dredge in cornmeal mixture.

Heat oil in a large nonstick skillet over medium heat. Add chicken, and cook 5 to 6 minutes on each side or until chicken is done. Serve with salsa.

Per Serving:

Calories 211	**Fiber** 1.5g
Fat 4.1g (sat 0.8g)	**Cholesterol** 66mg
Protein 29.5g	**Sodium** 337mg
Carbohydrate 12.6g	**Exchanges:** 1 Starch, 4 Very Lean Meat

Chicken Breast Dijon

Yield: 4 servings

⅓	cup fine, dry breadcrumbs
1	tablespoon Parmesan cheese
1	teaspoon dried Italian seasoning
½	teaspoon dried thyme
¼	teaspoon salt
¼	teaspoon freshly ground pepper
4	(4-ounce) skinned, boned chicken breast halves
2	tablespoons Dijon mustard
1	teaspoon olive oil
1	teaspoon reduced-calorie margarine

Combine first 6 ingredients in a small bowl, stirring well. Brush both sides of each chicken breast half with mustard; dredge in breadcrumb mixture.

Heat olive oil and margarine in a nonstick skillet over medium-high heat until margarine melts. Add chicken breasts, and cook 6 to 8 minutes on each side or until chicken is done.

Per Serving:

Calories 192	**Fiber** 0.5g
Fat 4.6g (sat 1.0g)	**Cholesterol** 67mg
Protein 27.9g	**Sodium** 553mg
Carbohydrate 7.5g	**Exchanges:** ½ Starch, 4 Very Lean Meat

Mustard-Parmesan Chicken

Yield: 4 servings

½   cup Italian-seasoned breadcrumbs
2   tablespoons grated Parmesan cheese
4   (4-ounce) skinned, boned chicken breast halves
3   tablespoons coarse-grained mustard
Cooking spray

Combine breadcrumbs and cheese in a small bowl, stirring well. Brush both sides of each chicken breast half with mustard; dredge in breadcrumb mixture.

Place chicken on rack of a broiler pan coated with cooking spray. Broil 5½ inches from heat 5 minutes on each side or until chicken is done. Serve immediately.

Per Serving:

Calories 180	**Fiber** 0.2g
Fat 3.6g (sat 1.1g)	**Cholesterol** 69mg
Protein 29.4g	**Sodium** 492mg
Carbohydrate 6.0g	**Exchanges:** ½ Starch, 4 Very Lean Meat

Grilled Caribbean Chicken

Yield: 4 servings

4   (4-ounce) skinned, boned chicken breast halves
2   teaspoons lime juice
1   teaspoon vegetable oil
2   teaspoons jerk seasoning
Cooking spray

Place chicken between 2 sheets of heavy-duty plastic wrap, and flatten to ¼-inch thickness, using a meat mallet or rolling pin. Combine lime juice and oil; brush over both sides of chicken. Rub both sides of chicken with jerk seasoning.

Coat grill rack with cooking spray; place rack on grill over medium-hot coals (350° to 400°). Place chicken on rack; grill, covered, 5 to 6 minutes on each side or until done. Serve over rice, if desired (rice not included in analysis).

Per Serving:

Calories 153	**Fiber** 0.2g
Fat 4.2g (sat 1.0g)	**Cholesterol** 70mg
Protein 25.9g	**Sodium** 97mg
Carbohydrate 1.4g	**Exchanges:** 4 Very Lean Meat

Chicken with Mushroom Sauce

Yield: 4 servings

1	teaspoon dried thyme
¼	teaspoon dried basil
⅛	teaspoon freshly ground pepper
4	(8-ounce) chicken leg quarters, skinned
Cooking spray	
⅓	cup dry white wine
⅓	cup low-sodium chicken broth
⅔	cup sliced fresh mushrooms
¼	cup shredded carrot
2	tablespoons all-purpose flour
2	tablespoons water
2	tablespoons fat-free sour cream

Combine first 3 ingredients; sprinkle evenly over chicken. Coat a nonstick skillet with cooking spray; place over medium heat until hot. Add chicken; cook 2 minutes on each side or until browned.

Add wine and broth to chicken; cover, reduce heat, and simmer 20 minutes. Add mushrooms and carrot; cover and simmer 10 minutes. Transfer chicken to a dish; set aside, and keep warm. Combine flour and water; stir well. Add to broth mixture in skillet; cook over medium heat, stirring constantly, until thickened. Stir in sour cream. Spoon evenly over chicken. Serve immediately.

Per Serving:

Calories 203	**Fiber** 0.5g
Fat 6.2g (sat 1.5g)	**Cholesterol** 108mg
Protein 28.9g	**Sodium** 133mg
Carbohydrate 5.7g	**Exchanges:** 4 Lean Meat

(Photograph on page 117)

Turkey Scaloppine with Tomatoes

Yield: 4 servings

½ cup fine, dry breadcrumbs
1 tablespoon chopped fresh basil or 1 teaspoon dried basil
¼ teaspoon garlic powder
¼ teaspoon ground pepper
⅛ teaspoon salt
1 pound turkey breast slices
2 large egg whites, lightly beaten
Olive oil-flavored cooking spray
1 teaspoon olive oil, divided
¼ cup dry vermouth
¼ cup fat-free, reduced-sodium chicken broth
1 teaspoon cornstarch
1 cup chopped tomato (about 1 small)

Combine first 5 ingredients in a small bowl; stir well. Dip each turkey slice in egg whites; dredge in breadcrumb mixture.

Coat a large nonstick skillet with cooking spray; add ½ teaspoon oil. Place over medium-high heat until hot. Add half of turkey slices; cook 2 to 3 minutes on each side or until turkey is done. Repeat procedure with remaining oil and turkey. Set aside, and keep warm.

Combine vermouth, broth, and cornstarch; stir. Add to skillet; cook over medium heat, stirring constantly, 1 minute or until slightly thickened. Add tomato; cook until thoroughly heated. Spoon over turkey. Serve immediately.

Per Serving:

Calories 191	**Fiber** 0.7g
Fat 3.5g (sat 0.8g)	**Cholesterol** 68mg
Protein 29.6g	**Sodium** 293mg
Carbohydrate 8.1g	**Exchanges:** 1 Vegetable, 4 Very Lean Meat

Turkey Enchiladas

Yield: 6 servings (serving size: 2 enchiladas)

1   pound ground turkey breast
2   cups salsa, divided
1   (10-ounce) package frozen chopped spinach, thawed and drained
1   (8-ounce) package fat-free cream cheese, cut into pieces
12 (6-inch) corn tortillas
Cooking spray
1   (14½-ounce) can no-salt-added diced tomatoes, undrained
1   teaspoon ground cumin
¾   cup (3 ounces) shredded reduced-fat Cheddar cheese
3   cups shredded iceberg lettuce
6   tablespoons fat-free sour cream

Cook turkey in a nonstick skillet over medium heat until browned, stirring until it crumbles. Add 1 cup salsa, spinach, and cream cheese. Cook until cheese melts. Remove from skillet. Wipe skillet dry; place over medium heat until hot. Coat both sides of tortillas with cooking spray. Place 1 tortilla in skillet. Cook 15 seconds on each side. Spoon ⅓ cup turkey mixture onto tortilla. Roll up; place, seam side down, in a 13- x 9-inch baking dish coated with cooking spray. Repeat with remaining tortillas and turkey.

Combine remaining salsa, tomato, and cumin; pour over tortillas. Bake, uncovered, at 350° for 25 minutes. Sprinkle with Cheddar cheese. Place ½ cup lettuce on each plate; place 2 enchiladas on lettuce. Top each serving with 1 tablespoon sour cream.

Per Serving:

Calories 349
Fat 6.0g (sat 2.6g)
Protein 34.2g
Carbohydrate 39.7g
Fiber 5.1g
Cholesterol 63mg
Sodium 883mg
Exchanges: 2 Starch, 1 Vegetable, 3 Lean Meat

Make Ahead!

Turkey-Mushroom Strata

Yield: 8 servings

5   (1.4-ounce) sourdough rolls
Cooking spray
1   pound turkey breakfast sausage
¾   cup (3 ounces) shredded Swiss cheese
1   (8-ounce) package sliced mushrooms
⅓   cup finely chopped onion
1½ cups fat-free milk
1   cup fat-free egg substitute
½   teaspoon ground pepper
¼   teaspoon salt
¼   teaspoon dry mustard

Cut rolls into 1-inch cubes; layer evenly in a 13- x 9-inch baking dish coated with cooking spray.

Cook turkey sausage in a nonstick skillet over medium-high heat until browned, stirring until it crumbles. Drain. Place sausage and cheese over bread cubes. Add mushrooms and onion to skillet; sauté 4 minutes or until tender. Spoon mushroom mixture over cheese in baking dish; set aside.

Combine milk and remaining 4 ingredients, stirring until smooth. Pour over mixture in baking dish. Cover and chill at least 8 hours.

Bake, uncovered, at 350° for 35 minutes or until a knife inserted in center comes out clean. Let stand 5 minutes before serving.

Per Serving:

Calories 240	**Fiber** 1.1g
Fat 10.3g (sat 4.0g)	**Cholesterol** 55mg
Protein 20.4g	**Sodium** 665mg
Carbohydrate 17.1g	**Exchanges:** 1 Starch, 3 Lean Meat

Salads

Romaine Salad with Fresh Strawberries, page 142

Yogurt-Topped Fruit Salad

Yield: 6 (½-cup) servings

1½ cups sliced fresh strawberries
2   small bananas, peeled and sliced
1   orange, peeled and sectioned
6   green leaf lettuce leaves
¼   cup vanilla low-fat yogurt sweetened with aspartame
1   tablespoon creamy peanut butter
1   tablespoon chopped roasted, salted peanuts

Combine first 3 ingredients in a bowl; and toss gently. Spoon ½ cup fruit mixture onto each of 6 lettuce-lined salad plates.

Combine yogurt and peanut butter, stirring well. Spoon yogurt mixture evenly over fruit. Sprinkle evenly with peanuts.

Per Serving:

Calories 89	**Fiber** 3.0g
Fat 3.0g (sat 0.6g)	**Cholesterol** 0mg
Protein 2.6g	**Sodium** 40mg
Carbohydrate 14.8g	**Exchanges:** 1 Fruit, ½ Fat

Orange-Avocado Salad

Yield: 6 servings

2   tablespoons fresh orange juice
2   tablespoons red wine vinegar
2   teaspoons olive oil
¼   teaspoon grated orange rind
⅛   teaspoon salt
⅛   teaspoon pepper
2   cups torn fresh watercress
1   cup torn fresh spinach
2   oranges, peeled and sectioned
1   small avocado, peeled and thinly sliced

Combine first 6 ingredients in a small bowl, stirring well with a wire whisk.

Combine watercress and spinach. Pour orange juice mixture over greens; toss gently.

Place watercress mixture evenly onto 6 salad plates. Arrange orange sections and avocado slices evenly over each salad.

Per Serving:

Calories 60	Fiber 1.9g
Fat 4.5g (sat 0.7g)	Cholesterol 0mg
Protein 1.1g	Sodium 63mg
Carbohydrate 5.1g	Exchanges: 1 Vegetable, 1 Fat

If you can't find watercress, use 2 more cups of torn fresh spinach.

Romaine Salad with Fresh Strawberries

Yield: 4 (1-cup) servings

4   cups torn romaine lettuce (about 1 small head)
1   cup quartered fresh strawberries
3   tablespoons fat-free raspberry vinaigrette

Combine lettuce and strawberries in a large bowl. Pour raspberry vinaigrette over lettuce mixture, and toss well.

Per Serving:

Calories 38

Fat 0.3g (sat 0.0g)

Protein 1.6g

Carbohydrate 8.0g

Fiber 2.4g

Cholesterol 0mg

Sodium 75mg

Exchange: 1 Vegetable

(Photograph on page 139)

For a refreshing springtime meal, serve this fruited salad with grilled herbed chicken breasts and steamed asparagus.

Mixed Greens with Parmesan Walnuts

Yield: 8 (2-cup) servings

¾ cup walnut pieces
Butter-flavored cooking spray
2 tablespoons grated fat-free Parmesan cheese
4 cups loosely packed torn iceberg lettuce
4 cups loosely packed torn leaf lettuce
4 cups loosely packed torn curly endive
4 cups loosely packed torn fresh spinach
½ cup fat-free balsamic vinaigrette

Place walnuts in an 8-inch square pan. Coat walnuts with cooking spray. Bake at 350° for 5 minutes. Sprinkle with cheese, tossing to coat. Bake 4 to 5 additional minutes or until cheese is lightly browned. Cool completely.

Combine iceberg lettuce and next 3 ingredients; toss. Drizzle with vinaigrette, and toss gently to coat. Top with walnuts.

Per Serving:

Calories 101	**Fiber** 1.9g
Fat 5.8g (sat 0.4g)	**Cholesterol** 0mg
Protein 3.5g	**Sodium** 270mg
Carbohydrate 9.5g	**Exchanges:** 2 Vegetable, 1 Fat

The toasted nuts add a wonderful crunch to this fresh mixed green salad.

Carrot-Cabbage Coleslaw

Yield: 4 (¹/₂-cup) servings

1¼   cups shredded cabbage
¾   cup shredded carrot
¼   cup grated Red Delicious apple
¼   cup crushed pineapple in juice, drained
¼   cup fat-free mayonnaise
1   tablespoon lemon juice
Cabbage leaves (optional)

Combine first 6 ingredients in a medium bowl; toss well. Cover and chill thoroughly.

To serve, spoon coleslaw into a cabbage-lined bowl, if desired.

Per Serving:

Calories 36	**Fiber** 1.3g
Fat 0.1g (sat 0.0g)	**Cholesterol** 0mg
Protein 0.5g	**Sodium** 198mg
Carbohydrate 8.8g	**Exchanges:** ½ Vegetable, ½ Fruit

Chilled Green Bean Salad

Yield: 4 servings

1   (9-ounce) package frozen French-style green beans
1   cup finely chopped tomato (about 1 medium)
1   cup thinly sliced cucumber (about 1 small)
⅓   cup finely chopped sweet red pepper
¼   cup fat-free Italian dressing
1   tablespoon dried parsley flakes

Cook green beans according to package directions, omitting salt; drain.

Place beans in a large bowl. Add tomato and remaining ingredients; toss gently. Cover and chill at least 2 hours.

Per Serving:

Calories 47	**Fiber** 3.0g
Fat 0.4g (sat 0.1g)	**Cholesterol** 0mg
Protein 2.0g	**Sodium** 170mg
Carbohydrate 10.4g	**Exchanges:** 2 Vegetable

Minted Cucumber Salad

Yield: 6 (1-cup) servings

½ cup vanilla low-fat yogurt
3 tablespoons chopped fresh mint
2 tablespoons white wine vinegar
2 teaspoons granulated sugar substitute (such as Splenda)
Dash of hot sauce
3 medium cucumbers, peeled and thinly sliced
1 small purple onion, sliced and separated into rings
Boston lettuce leaves (optional)

Combine first 5 ingredients in a small bowl; stir well.

Place cucumber and onion slices in a shallow dish. Spoon yogurt mixture over vegetables. Cover and chill at least 30 minutes. Serve over lettuce leaves, if desired.

Per Serving:

Calories 39	**Fiber** 1.4g
Fat 0.4g (sat 0.2g)	**Cholesterol** 1mg
Protein 1.9g	**Sodium** 18mg
Carbohydrate 7.5g	**Exchange:** 1 Vegetable

Sliced Tomato with Balsamic Vinaigrette

Yield: 4 servings

2	tablespoons balsamic vinegar
4	teaspoons chopped fresh basil
2	teaspoons olive oil
1	teaspoon Dijon mustard
2	small cloves garlic, crushed
2	large tomatoes, sliced
4	red leaf lettuce leaves
2	(¼-inch-thick) slice sweet onion, separated into rings

Combine first 5 ingredients; stir well with a wire whisk.

Arrange tomato slices evenly on 2 lettuce-lined plates. Arrange onion over tomato. Drizzle vinegar mixture evenly over salads.

Per Serving:

Calories 61	**Fiber** 2.3g
Fat 2.9g (sat 0.4g)	**Cholesterol** 0mg
Protein 1.6g	**Sodium** 52mg
Carbohydrate 8.8g	**Exchanges:** 1 Vegetable, ½ Fat

Life is too short to bother
with tasteless tomatoes.

CINDY PAWLCYN, American restaurateur and author

tomatoes

Broccoli-Corn Salad

Yield: 5 (1-cup) servings

2	(10-ounce) packages frozen broccoli flowerets
1	(15¼-ounce) can no-salt-added whole-kernel corn, drained
1	(4-ounce) jar diced pimiento, drained
¼	cup rice wine vinegar
1	tablespoon vegetable oil
¼	teaspoon salt
⅛	teaspoon pepper
⅛	teaspoon chili powder
⅛	teaspoon ground cumin
⅛	teaspoon dried oregano

Arrange broccoli in a steamer basket over boiling water. Cover and steam 5 to 6 minutes or until crisp-tender. Let cool.

Combine broccoli, corn, and pimiento in a large bowl. Combine vinegar and remaining 6 ingredients in a small bowl; stir well with a wire whisk. Pour vinegar mixture over broccoli mixture, and toss gently. Cover and chill.

Per Serving:

Calories 106	**Fiber** 3.3g
Fat 3.6g (sat 0.5g)	**Cholesterol** 0mg
Protein 5.0g	**Sodium** 142mg
Carbohydrate 15.8g	**Exchanges:** 1 Starch, 1 Fat

Baked Potato Salad

Yield: 6 (³/₄-cup) servings

4   (8-ounce) baking potatoes
³/₄   cup fat-free mayonnaise-type salad dressing (such as fat-free
        Miracle Whip)
¹/₃   cup minced onion
¹/₃   cup minced fresh parsley
¹/₄   cup fat-free sour cream
1   tablespoon cider vinegar
¹/₄   teaspoon salt
¹/₄   teaspoon pepper
1   large clove garlic, minced
Fresh parsley sprigs (optional)

Scrub potatoes; prick each several times with a fork. Bake at 400°
for 1 hour or until done. Let cool slightly; remove skin, if desired.

Cut potato into ¹/₂-inch cubes.

Combine salad dressing and next 7 ingredients in a medium bowl;
add cubed potato, and toss well. Cover and chill at least 2 hours.
Garnish with parsley sprigs, if desired.

Per Serving:

Calories 199	**Fiber** 3.0g
Fat 0.2g (sat 0.1g)	**Cholesterol** 0mg
Protein 4.1g	**Sodium** 398mg
Carbohydrate 45.7g	**Exchanges:** 3 Starch

Italian Pasta Salad

Yield: 6 (½-cup) servings

4	ounces tricolor rotini (corkscrew) pasta, uncooked
¾	cup (3 ounces) cubed part-skim mozzarella cheese
½	cup sliced zucchini
¼	cup chopped, seeded tomato
3	tablespoons fat-free Italian dressing
2	tablespoons white wine vinegar
¾	teaspoon minced garlic
½	teaspoon granulated sugar substitute (such as Splenda)
½	teaspoon Dijon mustard
¼	teaspoon pepper

Cook pasta according to package directions, omitting salt and fat. Drain; rinse with cold water, and drain. Add cheese, zucchini, and tomato, tossing gently.

Combine Italian dressing and remaining 5 ingredients, stirring well with a wire whisk. Add vinegar mixture to pasta mixture, and toss gently. Cover and chill 1 hour. Toss gently before serving.

Per Serving:

Calories 108	**Fiber** 0.9g
Fat 2.6g (sat 1.5g)	**Cholesterol** 8.2mg
Protein 5.8g	**Sodium** 162mg
Carbohydrate 14.9g	**Exchange:** 1 Starch

Make Ahead!

Tuna and Bow Tie Pasta Salad

Yield: 6 (1 1/2-cup) servings

8	ounces bow tie pasta, uncooked
1	(9-ounce) can solid white tuna in spring water, drained and flaked
1	cup finely chopped tomato (about 1 medium)
1/2	cup shredded carrot
1/2	cup finely chopped, unpeeled cucumber (about 1/2 small)
1/4	cup finely chopped celery
1/4	cup red wine vinegar
2	tablespoons water
1	tablespoon Dijon mustard
2	teaspoons olive oil
1/4	teaspoon ground pepper
1/8	teaspoon salt

Cook pasta according to package directions, omitting salt and fat. Drain; rinse under cold water, and drain again. Place pasta in a large bowl. Add tuna and next 4 ingredients.

Combine vinegar and remaining 5 ingredients in a small bowl, stirring well. Pour vinegar mixture over pasta mixture, and toss well. Cover and chill at least 2 hours. Toss gently before serving.

Per Serving:

Calories 218
Fat 3.3g (sat 0.5g)
Protein 14.8g
Carbohydrate 31.4g

Fiber 1.8g
Cholesterol 15mg
Sodium 274mg
Exchanges: 2 Starch, 1 Lean Meat

Tabbouleh-Vegetable Salad

Yield: 8 (1-cup) servings

1	cup bulgur (or cracked wheat), uncooked
2	cups fat-free, reduced-sodium chicken broth
3	cloves garlic, minced and divided
1	(15-ounce) can whole baby corn, drained
1	(14-ounce) can artichoke hearts, drained
1¼	cups sliced green onions
½	cup minced fresh mint
½	cup minced fresh parsley
¼	cup sliced ripe olives
¼	cup fat-free Italian dressing
3	tablespoons fresh lemon juice
5	dried tomatoes (packed in oil), drained and cut into thin strips
2	ounces crumbled feta cheese

Romaine lettuce leaves (optional)
Lemon slices (optional)

Combine bulgur, broth, and 1 minced garlic clove in a saucepan; bring to a boil. Cover, reduce heat, and simmer 15 minutes or until bulgur is tender and liquid is absorbed. Let cool.

Cut each ear of corn into thirds. Cut artichoke hearts into quarters. Combine corn, artichoke hearts, bulgur, remaining garlic, green onions, and next 7 ingredients in a large bowl; toss well. Cover and chill at least 2 hours. If desired, spoon mixture into a lettuce-lined serving bowl, and garnish with lemon slices.

Per Serving:

Calories 143	**Fiber** 5.8g
Fat 3.0g (sat 1.4g)	**Cholesterol** 6mg
Protein 5.9g	**Sodium** 462mg
Carbohydrate 25.1g	**Exchanges:** 1 Starch, 1 Vegetable, 1 Fat

Hoppin' John Salad

Yield: 6 (1-cup) servings

2 ½ cups low-sodium chicken broth, divided
1   cup converted rice, uncooked
¼   cup apple cider vinegar
1 ½ teaspoons salt-free Cajun seasoning
2   teaspoons olive oil
½   teaspoon dried thyme
½   teaspoon minced garlic
¼   teaspoon hot sauce
1   (15.8-ounce) can black-eyed peas, drained
½   cup finely chopped celery
½   cup thinly sliced green onions
3   (1-ounce) slices lean ham, cut into thin strips
Fresh thyme (optional)

Place 2 ¼ cups broth in a medium saucepan; bring to a boil. Add rice, stirring well. Cover, reduce heat, and simmer 20 minutes. Remove from heat; let stand, covered, 5 minutes.

Combine remaining ¼ cup broth, vinegar, and next 5 ingredients in a small bowl.

Combine rice, peas, and next 3 ingredients in a large bowl. Add vinegar mixture, stirring gently to combine. Cover and chill at least 30 minutes. Garnish with fresh thyme, if desired.

Per Serving:

Calories 227	Fiber 3.6g
Fat 3.7g (sat 0.5g)	Cholesterol 6mg
Protein 10.2g	Sodium 540mg
Carbohydrate 37.9g	Exchanges: 2 Starch, 1 Vegetable, ½ High-Fat Meat

What is more refreshing than
salads when your appetite
seems to have deserted you?

ALEXIS SOYER, French-born British chef

Shrimp and Spinach Salad

Yield: 4 servings

½ cup plain fat-free yogurt
½ cup fat-free mayonnaise-type salad dressing (such as fat-free Miracle Whip)
2 tablespoons grated orange rind
1 tablespoon crystallized ginger
2 tablespoons fresh orange juice
2 tablespoons lime juice
6 cups water
2 pounds medium-size fresh shrimp, peeled and deveined
1 pound torn fresh spinach
1 cup very thinly sliced jícama
16 teardrop cherry tomatoes, halved
1 medium papaya, peeled, seeded, and sliced
Lime zest (optional)
Lemon zest (optional)

Combine first 6 ingredients in container of an electric blender; cover and process until smooth, stopping once to scrape down sides. Chill.

Bring 6 cups water to a boil in a medium saucepan; add shrimp. Cook 3 to 5 minutes or until shrimp turn pink. Drain well; rinse with cold water. Cover and chill.

Divide spinach evenly among 4 salad plates. Arrange shrimp, jícama, tomato, and papaya evenly over spinach. Top with yogurt mixture. If desired, garnish with lime and lemon zest.

Per Serving:

Calories 216	Fiber 3.1g
Fat 1.7g (sat 0.4g)	Cholesterol 222mg
Protein 27.5g	Sodium 596mg
Carbohydrate 23.7g	Exchanges: 3 Vegetable, ½ Fruit, 3 Very Lean Meat

Curried Chicken Salad with Pineapple

Yield: 6 servings (serving size: about 1 cup)

Cooking spray
6   (4-ounce) skinned, boned chicken breast halves
2   tablespoons chopped almonds
1   (8-ounce) can pineapple tidbits in juice, undrained
¾   cup plain fat-free yogurt
1   teaspoon curry powder
¼   teaspoon salt
1   cup thinly sliced celery
5   red leaf lettuce leaves

Coat a large nonstick skillet with cooking spray; place over medium heat until hot. Add chicken; cook 7 minutes on each side or until done. Remove chicken from skillet; let cool slightly. Coarsely chop chicken.

Place small heavy skillet over medium-high heat until hot. Add almonds, and cook, stirring constantly, 1 minute or until toasted. Set almonds aside.

Drain pineapple tidbits, reserving 3 tablespoons juice. Combine reserved pineapple juice, yogurt, curry powder, and salt in a large bowl, stirring well. Add chicken, pineapple, and celery; toss well.

Spoon chicken salad evenly onto 5 individual lettuce-lined salad plates. Sprinkle evenly with almonds.

Per Serving:

Calories 192	Fiber 0.9g
Fat 4.7g (sat 1.0g)	Cholesterol 72mg
Protein 28.5g	Sodium 196mg
Carbohydrate 8.0g	Exchanges: ½ Fruit, 4 Very Lean Meat

Sides

Southern-Style Creamed Corn, page 166

Gingered Asparagus

Yield: 4 servings

1	pound fresh asparagus

Cooking spray

2	tablespoons low-sodium soy sauce
2	teaspoons sesame seeds, toasted
1	teaspoon minced fresh ginger

Dash of pepper

½	teaspoon grated orange rind

Snap off tough ends of asparagus. Remove scales from stalks with a knife or vegetable peeler, if desired. Cut spears into 2-inch pieces.

Coat a large nonstick skillet with cooking spray. Place over medium-low heat until hot. Add asparagus, soy sauce, sesame seeds, ginger, and pepper. Sauté 5 minutes or until asparagus is crisp-tender. To serve, transfer to a serving bowl, and sprinkle with orange rind.

Per Serving:

Calories 32	**Fiber** 1.8g
Fat 1.1g (sat 0.1g)	**Cholesterol** 0mg
Protein 2.6g	**Sodium** 244mg
Carbohydrate 4.6g	**Exchange:** 1 Vegetable

Roasted Green Beans and Onions

Yield: 4 (³/₄-cup) servings

1	pound fresh green beans, trimmed
1	small purple onion, sliced and separated into rings
4	large cloves garlic, cut in half lengthwise

Olive oil-flavored cooking spray
½ teaspoon dried thyme
¼ teaspoon salt
¼ teaspoon freshly ground pepper

Place beans, onion, and garlic in a 13- x 9-inch pan coated with cooking spray. Coat vegetables with cooking spray. Sprinkle vegetables with thyme, salt, and pepper; toss well.

Bake at 450° for 15 minutes or until tender, stirring once. Serve immediately.

Per Serving:

Calories 54	**Fiber** 2.5g
Fat 0.5g (sat 0.0g)	**Cholesterol** 0mg
Protein 2.5g	**Sodium** 156mg
Carbohydrate 11.8g	**Exchanges:** 2 Vegetable

Cauliflower with Cheese Sauce

Yield: 6 (1-cup) servings

1	medium cauliflower, broken into flowerets
1	tablespoon all-purpose flour
¾	cup fat-free milk, divided
⅛	teaspoon salt
⅛	teaspoon dry mustard
½	cup (2 ounces) shredded reduced-fat Cheddar cheese
2	tablespoons fat-free sour cream
2	tablespoons (½ ounce) shredded reduced-fat sharp Cheddar cheese

Cook cauliflower, covered, in a small amount of boiling water 8 to 10 minutes or until tender; drain. Place cauliflower in a serving dish; set aside, and keep warm.

Combine flour and ¼ cup milk; stir with a wire whisk until smooth. Combine flour mixture, remaining ½ cup milk, salt, and dry mustard in a small saucepan; stir well. Cook over medium heat, stirring constantly, until mixture is thickened and bubbly.

Add ½ cup cheese; cook over low heat, stirring until cheese melts. Remove from heat; stir in sour cream. Pour cheese sauce over cauliflower; sprinkle with 2 tablespoons cheese. Serve immediately.

Per Serving:

Calories 93	**Fiber** 4.6g
Fat 2.1g (sat 0.9g)	**Cholesterol** 6.8mg
Protein 8.6g	**Sodium** 188mg
Carbohydrate 12.5g	**Exchanges:** ½ Starch, 1 Vegetable, 1 Very Lean Meat

Southern-Style Creamed Corn

Yield: 4 (½-cup) servings

6   ears fresh corn
1   cup 1% low-fat milk, divided
2   teaspoons cornstarch
2   (½-inch-thick) onion slices
¼   teaspoon salt
¼   teaspoon pepper

Remove and discard husks and silks from corn. Cut corn from cobs, scraping cobs well to remove all milk. Set corn aside.

Combine ¼ cup milk and cornstarch; set aside. Combine remaining ¾ cup milk and onion in a large saucepan; bring to a boil over medium heat. Cover, reduce heat, and simmer 5 minutes; remove and discard onion.

Add corn to hot milk; bring to a boil. Reduce heat, and cook 5 minutes, stirring often. Add cornstarch mixture, salt, and pepper; cook, stirring constantly, 3 minutes or until thickened and bubbly. Serve immediately.

Per Serving:

Calories 144	**Fiber** 4.0g
Fat 1.9g (sat 0.6g)	**Cholesterol** 3mg
Protein 5.4g	**Sodium** 195mg
Carbohydrate 30.5g	**Exchanges:** 2 Starch

(Photograph on page 161)

Okra-Corn Creole

Yield: 12 (½-cup) servings

Cooking spray
1   cup chopped green pepper
½   cup chopped onion
2½   cups fresh corn cut from cob (about 3 ears)
½   cup water
2   (14½-ounce) cans no-salt-added whole tomatoes, undrained
         and chopped
2   tablespoons no-salt-added tomato paste
½   teaspoon granulated sugar substitute (such as Sugar Twin)
¼   teaspoon salt
¼   teaspoon pepper
¼   teaspoon hot sauce
2   cups sliced fresh okra

Coat a large nonstick skillet with cooking spray; place over medium-high heat until hot. Add green pepper and onion; sauté 3 minutes or until tender.

Add corn and water to vegetables in skillet, stirring well. Cover and cook over medium heat 5 minutes; stir gently, and cook 5 minutes. Add tomato and next 5 ingredients. Bring to a boil; cover, reduce heat, and simmer 10 minutes, stirring occasionally. Add okra; cover and simmer 5 to 7 minutes or until okra is tender.

Per Serving:

Calories 56	**Fiber** 1.9g
Fat 0.5g (sat 0.1g)	**Cholesterol** 0mg
Protein 2.2g	**Sodium** 67mg
Carbohydrate 12.3g	**Exchanges:** ½ Starch, 1 Vegetable

Ready in 20 Minutes!

Sugar Snap Peas with Papaya Salsa

Yield: 4 (1-cup) servings

1   cup peeled, seeded, and diced papaya
½   cup chopped fresh cilantro
1   tablespoon minced onion
2   teaspoons lime juice
2   teaspoons rice wine vinegar
⅛   teaspoon salt
⅛   teaspoon ground white pepper
1   pound fresh Sugar Snap peas, trimmed

Combine first 7 ingredients in a small bowl; toss gently, and set aside.

Arrange peas in a steamer basket over boiling water. Cover and steam 3 minutes or until peas are crisp-tender; drain well.

To serve, transfer peas to a serving bowl. Spoon papaya mixture over peas.

Per Serving:

Calories 68
Fat 0.3g (sat 0.1g)
Protein 3.5g
Carbohydrate 13.6g

Fiber 3.9g
Cholesterol 0mg
Sodium 82mg
Exchanges: 1 Vegetable, ½ Fruit

Spring Peas

Yield: 6 (¾-cup) servings

2   (10-ounce) packages frozen English peas
2   teaspoons reduced-calorie margarine
2   teaspoons lemon juice
1½ teaspoons finely chopped fresh thyme
        or ½ teaspoon dried thyme
¼   teaspoon salt
⅛   teaspoon ground pepper

Cook peas according to package directions, omitting salt; drain and transfer to a large bowl.

Add margarine and remaining 4 ingredients, stirring until margarine melts. Serve warm.

Per Serving:

Calories 80	**Fiber** 4.3g
Fat 1.2g (sat 0.2g)	**Cholesterol** 0mg
Protein 4.9g	**Sodium** 216mg
Carbohydrate 13.1g	**Exchanges:** 2 Vegetable

These tasty, tender peas are wonderful with roasted lamb and steamed new potatoes.

Cheese Fries

Yield: 6 servings

2   tablespoons grated Parmesan cheese
½   teaspoon paprika
½   teaspoon salt
¼   teaspoon ground pepper
½   (32-ounce) bag frozen crinkle-cut French-fried potatoes
Cooking spray

Combine first 4 ingredients in a small bowl, stirring well; set aside.

Place French fries in a medium bowl; coat with cooking spray. Sprinkle fries with cheese mixture, tossing well.

Arrange French fries in a single layer on a baking sheet coated with cooking spray. Bake at 450° for 13 minutes or until tender. Serve immediately.

Per Serving:

Calories 139	Fiber 1.9g
Fat 3.9g (sat 1.2g)	Cholesterol 1mg
Protein 2.6g	Sodium 245mg
Carbohydrate 21.3g	Exchanges: 1 Starch, 1 Fat

Fruited Acorn Squash

Yield: 4 servings

2   medium acorn squash (about 1 pound each)
Cooking spray
⅓   cup drained canned pineapple tidbits in juice
⅓   cup peeled, chopped orange
2   tablespoons granulated brown sugar substitute (such as brown
        Sugar Twin)
2   tablespoons chopped pecans
¼   teaspoon salt

Cut each squash in half crosswise; remove and discard seeds. Place squash halves, cut sides down, in a 15- x 10-inch jellyroll pan coated with cooking spray. Bake, uncovered, at 350° for 35 minutes or until squash is tender.

Combine pineapple and remaining 4 ingredients; spoon mixture evenly into squash halves. Bake, uncovered, 10 minutes or until thoroughly heated.

Per Serving:

Calories 120	**Fiber** 3.1g
Fat 2.8g (sat 0.2g)	**Cholesterol** 0mg
Protein 1.9g	**Sodium** 160mg
Carbohydrate 24.9g	**Exchanges:** 1 Starch, ½ Fruit

The tender flesh of the squash absorbs the brown-sugared sweetness of pineapple and orange as the squash bakes.

Mexican Spaghetti Squash

Yield: 8 (½-cup) servings

1   (3-pound) spaghetti squash
Cooking spray
½   cup chopped onion
1   small clove garlic, minced
1   cup chopped tomato
2   tablespoons canned chopped green chiles
¼   teaspoon chili powder
⅛   teaspoon ground cumin
⅛   teaspoon ground red pepper

Wash squash; cut in half lengthwise. Remove and discard seeds. Place squash, cut sides down, in a Dutch oven; add water to pan to a depth of 2 inches. Bring to a boil; cover, reduce heat, and simmer 20 to 25 minutes or until squash is tender. Drain squash, and let cool.

Using a fork, remove spaghetti-like strands from squash; discard shells. Set squash aside.

Coat a large nonstick skillet with cooking spray; place over medium-high heat until hot. Add onion and garlic; sauté 3 to 4 minutes or until tender. Stir in tomato and remaining 4 ingredients; cook until thoroughly heated. Add squash; cook until thoroughly heated, stirring occasionally. Serve warm.

Per Serving:

Calories 38	**Fiber** 1.8g
Fat 0.4g (sat 0.1g)	**Cholesterol** 0mg
Protein 1.0g	**Sodium** 25mg
Carbohydrate 8.3g	**Exchanges:** 2 Vegetable

Seasoned Couscous

Yield: 4 (½-cup) servings

Cooking spray
½   teaspoon peanut oil
¼   cup sliced green onions
¾   cup water
1   teaspoon chicken-flavored bouillon granules
½   cup uncooked couscous
2   teaspoons low-sodium soy sauce
⅓   cup peeled, seeded, and chopped tomato
1   tablespoon chopped fresh parsley
⅓   teaspoon freshly ground pepper
1   Roma tomato (optional)
½   teaspoon whole peppercorns (optional)

Coat a saucepan with cooking spray; add oil. Place over medium-high heat until hot. Add green onions, and sauté until tender.

Add water and bouillon granules; bring to a boil. Remove from heat. Add couscous and soy sauce; cover and let stand 5 minutes. Stir in chopped tomato, parsley, and pepper.

To garnish, cut top third from Roma tomato, if desired; discard top. Use a paring knife to make decorative cuts around edge of tomato; place peppercorns in center, if desired.

Per Serving:

Calories 97	Fiber 0.7g
Fat 1.0g (sat 0.2g)	Cholesterol 0mg
Protein 3.3g	Sodium 275mg
Carbohydrate 18.5g	Exchanges: 1 Starch, 1 Vegetable

Green Onion Rice

Yield: 6 (½-cup) servings

2¾ cups cooked instant long-grain rice (cooked without salt or fat)
½   cup chopped green onions
½   teaspoon salt
¼   teaspoon curry powder
¼   teaspoon ground cumin
¼   teaspoon freshly ground pepper
Cooking spray

Place first 6 ingredients in a large skillet coated with cooking spray. Sauté over medium-high heat 3 to 5 minutes or until mixture is thoroughly heated.

Per Serving:

Calories 103	**Fiber** 0.7g
Fat 0.2g (sat 0.0g)	**Cholesterol** 0mg
Protein 2.0g	**Sodium** 198mg
Carbohydrate 22.8g	**Exchanges:** 1½ Starch

Broccoli-Rice Timbales

Yield: 6 servings

1   (10-ounce) package frozen chopped broccoli
Cooking spray
½   cup chopped onion
1   clove garlic, minced
2   cups cooked short-grain rice (cooked without salt or fat)
½   teaspoon salt
Pimiento strips (optional)

Cook broccoli according to package directions, omitting salt.
Drain well, and set aside.

Coat a large nonstick skillet with cooking spray; place over
medium-high heat until hot. Add onion and garlic; sauté until
tender. Stir in broccoli, rice, and salt. Cook until thoroughly
heated, stirring frequently.

Pack evenly into 6 (6-ounce) custard cups coated with cooking spray.
Invert onto plates (see photo); garnish with pimiento, if desired.

Per Serving:

Calories 94	**Fiber** 1.8g
Fat 0.5g (sat 0.1g)	**Cholesterol** 0mg
Protein 3.0g	**Sodium** 207mg
Carbohydrate 19.8g	**Exchanges:** 1 Starch, 1 Vegetable

Inverting Timbales

Cracked Pepper Linguine

Yield: 6 (¾-cup) servings

8	ounces linguine, uncooked
¼	cup minced onion
2	cloves garlic, minced
1	tablespoon reduced-calorie margarine, melted
1	(8-ounce) carton fat-free sour cream
1	tablespoon fat-free milk
1	tablespoon cracked pepper
2	tablespoons freshly grated Parmesan cheese
1½	tablespoons chopped fresh parsley

Cook linguine according to package directions, omitting salt and fat. Drain. Set aside, and keep warm.

Sauté onion and garlic in margarine in a small skillet over medium heat until onion is crisp-tender.

Combine sour cream, milk, and pepper in a small bowl; stir well.

Combine pasta, onion mixture, and sour cream mixture; toss well. Sprinkle with Parmesan cheese and parsley. Serve immediately.

Per Serving:

Calories 193	**Fiber** 1.4g
Fat 2.4g (sat 0.6g)	**Cholesterol** 1mg
Protein 8.6g	**Sodium** 82mg
Carbohydrate 32.8g	**Exchanges:** 2 Starch, ½ Fat

Fresh Pepper Pasta

Yield: 6 (1-cup) servings

4	medium-size sweet red peppers (about 1½ pounds), seeded and chopped
2	tablespoons dry white wine or low-sodium chicken broth
¾	cup drained canned navy beans
½	cup thinly sliced green onions
⅓	cup shredded fresh basil leaves
1	tablespoon minced fresh oregano
1	tablespoon chopped ripe olives
6	ounces rotini pasta, uncooked
¼	cup plus 2 tablespoons (1½ ounces) shredded Asiago cheese
1	tablespoon pine nuts, toasted

Combine red pepper and wine in a saucepan; bring to a boil. Cover, reduce heat, and simmer 3 minutes.

Stir in beans and next 4 ingredients; bring to a boil. Cover, reduce heat, and simmer 10 minutes. Uncover and simmer 20 minutes, stirring occasionally.

Cook pasta according to package directions, omitting salt and fat. Drain well.

Place pasta evenly on individual serving plates. Top evenly with pepper mixture, cheese, and pine nuts.

Per Serving:

Calories 189	Fiber 3.2g
Fat 3.8g (sat 1.3g)	Cholesterol 4mg
Protein 8.5g	Sodium 196mg
Carbohydrate 31.5g	Exchanges: 2 Starch, ½ Fat

Soups & Sandwiches

Fiesta Burgers, page 193

Spicy Pepper Soup

Yield: 7 (1-cup) servings

2	cups chopped sweet red pepper
2	cups peeled, cubed potato
¾	cup chopped purple onion
2	cups water
1	(16-ounce) can tomato sauce
½	cup dry white vermouth or low-sodium chicken broth
¼	cup chopped fresh cilantro
½	teaspoon ground cumin
½	teaspoon ground red pepper
⅛	teaspoon ground cinnamon
¼	cup plus 3 tablespoons fat-free sour cream
	Chopped fresh cilantro (optional)
	Chopped purple onion (optional)
	Chopped sweet red pepper (optional)

Combine first 4 ingredients in a Dutch oven; bring to a boil. Cover, reduce heat, and simmer 20 minutes or until vegetables are tender.

Add tomato sauce and next 5 ingredients to Dutch oven; bring to a boil, stirring occasionally. Reduce heat, and simmer, uncovered, 10 minutes.

Process mixture, in batches, in container of an electric blender until smooth. Ladle soup into individual bowls; top each serving with 1 tablespoon sour cream. If desired, top with cilantro, chopped onion, and chopped pepper.

Per Serving:

Calories 106	Fiber 2.9g
Fat 0.5g (sat 0.1g)	Cholesterol 0mg
Protein 3.5g	Sodium 411mg
Carbohydrate 19.1g	Exchanges: 1 Starch, 1 Vegetable

Cheddar Potato Soup

Yield: 7 (1-cup) servings

2 (16-ounce) cans fat-free, reduced-sodium chicken broth
5 cups frozen shredded potato
1 cup frozen chopped onion
½ teaspoon salt
½ teaspoon ground pepper
2 tablespoons all-purpose flour
1 (12-ounce) can fat-free evaporated milk
1 cup (4 ounces) shredded reduced-fat sharp Cheddar cheese
⅓ cup chopped green onions

Combine first 5 ingredients in a Dutch oven; bring to a boil. Reduce heat, and simmer, uncovered, 20 minutes.

Combine flour and milk, stirring until smooth. Add to potato mixture. Cook over medium heat, stirring constantly, 5 minutes or until thickened.

Pour half of potato mixture into container of an electric blender; cover and process until smooth. Pour into a large bowl. Repeat procedure with remaining half of potato mixture.

Return mixture to Dutch oven. Add cheese; cook over medium heat, stirring until cheese melts. Ladle soup into individual bowls; sprinkle evenly with green onions.

Per Serving:

Calories 158

Fat 3.2g (sat 1.9g)

Protein 10.6g

Carbohydrate 17.3g

Fiber 1.2g

Cholesterol 13mg

Sodium 623mg

Exchanges: 1 Starch, 1 Lean Meat

Five-Ingredient Chili

Yield: 14 (1-cup) servings

1½ pounds ground round
1 medium onion, chopped
4 (16-ounce) cans chili-hot beans, undrained
1 (1¾-ounce) package chili seasoning mix
1 (46-ounce) can no-salt-added tomato juice

Cook meat and onion in a Dutch oven over medium-high heat until meat is browned, stirring until it crumbles; drain, if necessary. Stir in beans and remaining ingredients.

Bring to a boil; reduce heat, and simmer, uncovered, 30 minutes or to desired consistency, stirring occasionally.

Per Serving:

Calories 220	**Fiber** 6.2g
Fat 3.9g (sat 1.6g)	**Cholesterol** 30mg
Protein 17.8g	**Sodium** 803mg
Carbohydrate 26.1g	**Exchanges:** 1 Starch, 2 Vegetable, 2 Lean Meat

With only five ingredients and a 10-minute prep time, this hot-and-spicy chili is one of our favorites.

Harvest Stew

Yield: 8 (1¼-cup) servings

Cooking spray
1   pound ground round
¾   cup chopped onion
½   teaspoon pepper
2   cloves garlic, minced
3½ cups water
1   (14½-ounce) can no-salt-added diced tomatoes, undrained
2¼ cups peeled, chopped sweet potato
1   cup unpeeled, coarsely chopped round red potato
1   cup peeled, chopped acorn squash
2   teaspoons vegetable-flavored bouillon granules
½   teaspoon chili powder
¼   teaspoon ground allspice
¼   teaspoon ground cloves
2   bay leaves

Coat a Dutch oven with cooking spray; place over medium-high heat until hot. Add meat and next 3 ingredients. Cook until meat is browned, stirring until it crumbles. Drain, if necessary.

Combine meat mixture, water, and remaining ingredients in Dutch oven; bring to a boil. Cover, reduce heat, and simmer 30 minutes or until vegetables are tender. Remove and discard bay leaves before serving.

Per Serving:

Calories 156	Fiber 2.3g
Fat 3.9g (sat 1.4g)	Cholesterol 36mg
Protein 12.4g	Sodium 163mg
Carbohydrate 19.6g	Exchanges: 1 Starch, 1 Vegetable, 1 Lean Meat

Hearty Pork Stew

Yield: 8 (1-cup) servings

Cooking spray
1   pound lean boneless pork loin, cut into cubes
1   cup chopped onion
1   (14½-ounce) can no-salt-added diced tomatoes, undrained
2   cups low-sodium chicken broth
1   (10-ounce) package frozen baby lima beans
1   (10-ounce) package frozen whole-kernel corn
1   (4.5-ounce) can chopped green chiles
½   teaspoon salt
½   teaspoon hot sauce
¼   teaspoon garlic powder
¼   teaspoon onion powder
¼   teaspoon freshly ground pepper
2   tablespoons all-purpose flour
2   tablespoons water

Coat a Dutch oven with cooking spray; place over medium-high heat until hot. Add pork and onion; cook 5 minutes or until pork is browned, stirring frequently. Drain; pat dry.

Return pork to Dutch oven; add tomato and next 9 ingredients. Bring to a boil; cover, reduce heat, and simmer 40 minutes.

Combine flour and water; stir until smooth; add to stew. Cook, stirring constantly, until thickened.

Per Serving:

Calories 211	**Fiber** 2.4g
Fat 6.6g (sat 2.2g)	**Cholesterol** 37mg
Protein 16.5g	**Sodium** 258mg
Carbohydrate 22.7g	**Exchanges:** 1 Starch, 2 Vegetable, 1 Medium-Fat Meat

Chicken-Chili Stew

Yield: 8 (2-cup servings)

1   (16-ounce) can fat-free, reduced-sodium chicken broth
1   (15-ounce) can chunky chili tomato sauce, undrained
1   (4.5-ounce) can chopped green chiles
1½ cups frozen chopped onion
1   cup frozen whole-kernel corn
2   tablespoons chili powder
1   (15-ounce) can kidney beans, drained
¾   pound skinned, boned chicken breast halves, cut into 1-inch pieces
¼   cup chopped fresh cilantro or parsley

Combine first 6 ingredients in a Dutch oven. Bring to a boil; cover, reduce heat, and simmer 10 minutes.

Add beans and chicken; cover and simmer 10 additional minutes. Remove from heat; add cilantro. Serve immediately.

Per Serving:

Calories 147

Fat 1.0g (sat 0.2g)

Protein 14.0g

Carbohydrate 19.9g

Fiber 3.9g

Cholesterol 25mg

Sodium 523mg

Exchanges: 1 Starch, 1 Vegetable, 1 Very Lean Meat

Creole Shrimp Stew

Yield: 4 (1-cup) servings

Cooking spray
1 teaspoon vegetable oil
½ cup chopped onion
½ cup chopped celery
½ teaspoon salt
1½ teaspoons minced fresh thyme or ½ teaspoon dried thyme
¼ teaspoon ground pepper
2 tablespoons dry red wine
1 (14½-ounce) can no-salt-added diced tomatoes, undrained
6 ounces peeled and deveined medium-size fresh shrimp
6 ounces halibut fillets, cut into bite-size pieces

Coat a Dutch oven with cooking spray; add oil. Place over medium-high heat until hot. Add onion and next 4 ingredients; sauté 5 minutes. Add wine and tomato. Bring to a boil; reduce heat, and simmer, uncovered, 5 minutes.

Add shrimp and halibut to Dutch oven. Cover and simmer 5 additional minutes or until shrimp turn pink and fish flakes easily when tested with a fork. Serve immediately.

Per Serving:

Calories 132	**Fiber** 1.4g
Fat 3.0g (sat 0.5g)	**Cholesterol** 85mg
Protein 18.7g	**Sodium** 406mg
Carbohydrate 7.3g	**Exchanges:** 1 Vegetable, 2 Very Lean Meat

Sloppy Joes

Yield: 8 servings

1½ pounds ground round
1   cup chopped onion
½   cup chopped green pepper
1   cup ketchup
1   (8-ounce) can no-salt-added tomato sauce
1½ tablespoons low-sodium Worcestershire sauce
1½ tablespoons lemon juice
1½ tablespoons prepared mustard
2   teaspoons granulated brown sugar substitute (such as Brown Sugar
        Twin)
¼   teaspoon garlic powder
¼   teaspoon pepper
8   hamburger buns

Cook meat, onion, and green pepper in a large nonstick skillet over medium-high heat until meat is browned, stirring until it crumbles. Drain, if necessary.

Add ketchup and next 7 ingredients; stir well. Cook, uncovered, over medium heat 10 minutes or until thoroughly heated and slightly thickened, stirring frequently.

Spoon meat mixture evenly over bottom halves of buns. Top with remaining bun halves.

Per Serving:

Calories 306	**Fiber** 2.0g
Fat 7.8g (sat 2.5g)	**Cholesterol** 54mg
Protein 23.5g	**Sodium** 694mg
Carbohydrate 35.3g	**Exchanges:** 2 Starch, 1 Vegetable, 2 Medium-Fat Meat

Fiesta Burgers

Yield: 8 servings

1⅓   cups seeded, chopped tomato
¼   cup finely chopped onion
¼   cup taco sauce
1   (4.5-ounce) can chopped green chiles, drained
2   pounds ground round
2   tablespoons low-sodium Worcestershire sauce
½   teaspoon ground cumin
¼   teaspoon onion powder
¼   teaspoon garlic powder
8   green leaf lettuce leaves
8   reduced-calorie hamburger buns, split and toasted

Combine first 4 ingredients; cover and chill 30 minutes.

Combine meat and next 4 ingredients; divide mixture into 8 equal portions, shaping each into a 4-inch patty. Broil 3 inches from heat 4 minutes on each side or until done.

Place a lettuce leaf on bottom half of each bun; top each with a patty. Top evenly with tomato mixture, and cover with bun tops.

Per Serving:

Calories 266	**Fiber** 2.6g
Fat 8.0g (sat 2.5g)	**Cholesterol** 70mg
Protein 26.8g	**Sodium** 423mg
Carbohydrate 19.7g	**Exchanges:** 1 Starch, 1 Vegetable, 3 Lean Meat

(Photograph on page 181)

Italian Meatball Sandwich

Yield: 6 servings

6   (2-ounce) whole wheat submarine loaves
1   pound ground round
¼   cup finely chopped onion
3   tablespoons Italian-seasoned breadcrumbs
2   tablespoons water
¼   teaspoon pepper
1   large egg white, lightly beaten
1½   cups low-fat, reduced-sodium pasta sauce
¾   cup (3 ounces) shredded part-skim mozzarella cheese
Fresh basil sprigs (optional)

Cut an oval piece out of top of each loaf. Reserve oval pieces for another use.

Combine meat and next 5 ingredients; stir. Shape into 36 (1-inch) balls. Cook meatballs in a large nonstick skillet over medium heat 8 to 10 minutes or until browned on all sides. Remove from heat, and pat dry.

Return meatballs to skillet; add pasta sauce. Cook over medium-low heat 10 minutes or until thoroughly heated.

Place loaves on a baking sheet; top each with 6 meatballs. Spoon sauce evenly over meatballs. Sprinkle evenly with cheese. Bake at 400° for 5 minutes or until cheese melts. Garnish with basil sprigs, if desired.

Per Serving:

Calories 269	Fiber 1.2g
Fat 7.6g (sat 2.4g)	Cholesterol 60mg
Protein 25.8g	Sodium 621mg
Carbohydrate 23.4g	Exchanges: 1½ Starch, 3 Lean Meat

Lamb Pockets with Cucumber Topping

Yield: 8 servings (serving size: ½ pita)

1	cup grated cucumber
½	cup plain low-fat yogurt
¼	teaspoon seasoned salt
¼	teaspoon dried dillweed
1	pound ground lamb or ground round
¼	cup chopped onion
1	clove garlic, minced
¼	teaspoon salt
¼	teaspoon pepper
¾	cup chopped tomato
¼	cup sliced green onions
4	(6-inch) whole wheat pita bread rounds, cut in half crosswise
8	green leaf lettuce leaves

Press cucumber between layers of paper towels to remove excess moisture. Combine cucumber, yogurt, seasoned salt, and dillweed; cover and chill.

Cook meat, chopped onion, and garlic in a large nonstick skillet over medium-high heat until meat is browned, stirring until it crumbles. Drain, if necessary. Stir in ¼ teaspoon salt and pepper. Set aside.

Combine tomato and green onions. Line each pita half with a lettuce leaf; top evenly with meat mixture, cucumber mixture, and tomato mixture. Serve immediately.

Per Serving:

Calories 195	Fiber 1.3g
Fat 4.9g (sat 1.7g)	Cholesterol 41mg
Protein 16.8g	Sodium 346mg
Carbohydrate 20.0g	Exchanges: 1 Starch, 1 Vegetable, 2 Lean Meat

Turkey-Roasted Pepper Sandwiches

Yield: 4 sandwiches

2   tablespoons fat-free cream cheese, softened
1   tablespoon reduced-fat mayonnaise
1   tablespoon spicy brown mustard
⅛   teaspoon pepper
¼   cup roasted red peppers in water, drained and chopped
2   tablespoons sliced green onions
8   slices pumpernickel bread
¾   pound thinly sliced smoked turkey breast
¼   cup alfalfa sprouts
4   leaf lettuce leaves

Combine first 4 ingredients, stirring until smooth. Stir in red peppers and green onions.

Spread 1 side of bread slices evenly with cream cheese mixture.

Top 4 bread slices evenly with turkey, sprouts, and lettuce leaves. Top with remaining bread slices.

Per Sandwich:

Calories 296	**Fiber** 4.1g
Fat 3.0g (sat 0.6g)	**Cholesterol** 74mg
Protein 32.9g	**Sodium** 596mg
Carbohydrate 34.9g	**Exchanges:** 2 Starch, 1 Vegetable, 3 Very Lean Meat

7-DAY MENU PLANNER

Explanation of Menus

Use these menus and the recipes in the book to make your meal plan work for you. Since meal and snack plans differ according to dietary treatments and goals, this weekly menu planner is simply a guide to recipes and food items that make pleasing meals. Use your own meal plan to determine the number of servings you can have or the number of other items you can add to your meal.

Page numbers are provided for you to refer to the recipes in the book. The other items are listed to round out the meal; substitute as desired. Start with this menu plan for ideas and then create your own meal plans using other recipes in the book.

Day 1

BREAKFAST
Blueberry Bran Muffins (page 31)
Scrambled egg
Orange juice

LUNCH
Tuna and Bow Tie Pasta Salad (page 153)
Orange-Avocado Salad (page 141)

DINNER
Turkey Enchiladas (page 137)
Shredded lettuce
Pineapple slices

SNACK
Peanut butter
Graham crackers

Day 2

BREAKFAST
Whole Wheat Biscuits (page 37)
Fresh strawberries
Fat-free milk

LUNCH
Turkey-Roasted Pepper Sandwiches (page 197)
Low-fat potato chips
Cantaloupe wedge

DINNER
Sweet-and-Sour Shrimp (page 76)
Rice
Minted Cucumber Salad (page 147)

SNACK
Turkey-Spinach Pinwheels (page 19)

Day 3

BREAKFAST
Whole wheat
English muffin with low-sugar jelly
Orange juice
Fat-free milk

LUNCH
French Bread Pizza (page 92)
Carrot and celery sticks
Orange

DINNER
Quick-and-Easy Salisbury Steaks (page 99)
Low-fat mashed potatoes (from frozen)
Steamed green peas

SNACK
Rocky Road Fudge Pops (page 54)

Day 4

BREAKFAST
Bagel with ⅓-less fat
cream cheese
Fresh strawberries

LUNCH
**Sesame Broccoli
Stir-Fry
(page 93)**
Rice noodles
Orange wedges

DINNER
**Skillet Chops
and Rice
(page 113)**
Steamed green
beans
Applesauce

SNACK
**Fudgy Cream
Cheese Brownie
(page 60)**
Fat-free milk

Day 5

BREAKFAST
**Strawberry
Bread (page 36)**
Vanilla low-fat
yogurt

LUNCH
**Artichoke Quiche
(page 84)**
Breadsticks
Apple

DINNER
**Crispy Cornmeal
Chicken
(page 128)**
**Carrot-Cabbage
Coleslaw
(page 144)**
Tomato slices
Melon balls

SNACK
**Frosted
Cappuccino
(page 24)**

Day 6

BREAKFAST
**Cheddar-Potato
Frittata
(page 83)**
Whole wheat toast
Grapefruit sections

LUNCH
**Five-Ingredient
Chili (page 185)**
Saltine crackers
Apple

DINNER
**Roasted Lamb
and Vegetables
(page 109)**
French bread
Pear slices

SNACK
**Peanut Butter-
and-Jelly
Sandwich
Cookies
(page 58)**
Fat-free milk

Day 7

BREAKFAST
**Cherry
Coffee Cake
(page 40)**
Orange sections
Fat-free milk

LUNCH
**Sloppy Joes
(page 192)**
Low-fat potato chips
Mixed fruit salad

DINNER
**Veal Parmesan
with Tomato
Salsa (page 108)**
Spaghetti noodles
Mixed greens with
fat-free vinaigrette

SNACK
Low-fat snack mix
Fat-free milk

Nutrition Notes

Delicious Ways to Control Diabetes gives you the nutrition facts you want to know. We provide the following information with every recipe.

values are for one serving of the recipe

Per Serving:

Calories 299

Fat 2.0g (sat 0.4g)

Protein 22.8g

Carbohydrate 29.1g

Fiber 2.0 g — grams are abbreviated "g"

Cholesterol 47 mg — milligrams are abbreviated "mg"

Sodium 644mg

Exchanges: 2 Starch, 2 Medium-Fat Meat — exchange values are for one serving

total carbohydrate in one serving

Nutritional Analyses

The nutritional values used in our calculations either come from a nutrient analysis computer program or are provided by food manufacturers. The values are based on the following assumptions:

- When we give a range for an ingredient, we calculate using the lesser amount.
- Only the amount of marinade absorbed is calculated.
- Garnishes and optional ingredients are not included in the analysis.

Diabetic Exchanges

Exchange values for all recipes are provided for people who use them for meal planning. The exchange values in this book are based on the *Exchange Lists for Meal Planning* developed by the American Diabetes Association and The American Dietetic Association.

Carbohydrate

If you count carbohydrate, look for the value in the nutrient analysis. New American Diabetes Association guidelines loosen the restriction on sugar and encourage you to look at the total grams of carbohydrate in a serving. We have used small amounts of sugar in some recipes. We have also used a variety of sugar substitutes when the use of a substitute yields a quality product (see the Sugar Substitute Guide on page 10).

Sodium

Current dietary recommendations advise a daily sodium intake of 2,400 milligrams. We have limited the sodium in these recipes by using reduced-sodium products whenever possible.

If you must restrict sodium in your diet, please note the sodium value per serving and see if you should further modify the recipe.

Recipe Index

See page 206 for Quick and Easy Recipes.

Quick and Easy Recipes

Metric Equivalents

The recipes that appear in this cookbook use the standard United States method for measuring liquid and dry or solid ingredients (teaspoons, tablespoons, and cups). The information in the following charts is provided to help cooks outside the U.S. successfully use these recipes. All equivalents are approximate.

Equivalents for Different Types of Ingredients

A standard cup measure of a dry or solid ingredient will vary in weight depending on the type of ingredient. A standard cup of liquid is the same volume for any type of liquid. Use the following chart when converting standard cup measures to grams (weight) or milliliters (volume).

Standard Cup	Fine Powder (ex. flour)	Grain (ex. rice)	Granular (ex. sugar)	Liquid Solids (ex. butter)	Liquid (ex. milk)
1	140 g	150 g	190 g	200 g	240 ml
¾	105 g	113 g	143 g	150 g	180 ml
⅔	93 g	100 g	125 g	133 g	160 ml
½	70 g	75 g	95 g	100 g	120 ml
⅓	47 g	50 g	63 g	67 g	80 ml
¼	35 g	38 g	48 g	50 g	60 ml
⅛	18 g	19 g	24 g	25 g	30 ml

Dry Ingredients by Weight

(To convert ounces to grams, multiply the number of ounces by 30.)

1 oz	=	1/16 lb	=	30 g
4 oz	=	¼ lb	=	120 g
8 oz	=	½ lb	=	240 g
12 oz	=	¾ lb	=	360 g
16 oz	=	1 lb	=	480 g

Length

(To convert inches to centimeters, multiply the number of inches by 2.5.)

1 in	=				2.5 cm	
6 in	=	½ ft		=	15 cm	
12 in	=	1 ft		=	30 cm	
36 in	=	3 ft	= 1 yd =	90 cm	
40 in	=				100 cm	= 1 m

Liquid Ingredients by Volume

¼ tsp						1 ml	
½ tsp						2 ml	
1 tsp						5 ml	
3 tsp	=	1 tbls		=	½ fl oz	=	15 ml
		2 tbls	= ⅛ cup	=	1 fl oz	=	30 ml
		4 tbls	= ¼ cup	=	2 fl oz	=	60 ml
		5⅓ tbls	= ⅓ cup	=	3 fl oz	=	80 ml
		8 tbls	= ½ cup	=	4 fl oz	=	120 ml
		10⅔ tbls	= ⅔ cup	=	5 fl oz	=	160 ml
		12 tbls	= ¾ cup	=	6 fl oz	=	180 ml
		16 tbls	= 1 cup	=	8 fl oz	=	240 ml
		1 pt	= 2 cups	=	16 fl oz	=	480 ml
		1 qt	= 4 cups	=	32 fl oz	=	960 ml
					33 fl oz	=	1000 ml = 1 liter

Cooking/Oven Temperatures

	Fahrenheit	Celsius	Gas Mark
Freeze Water	32° F	0° C	
Room Temperature	68° F	20° C	
Boil Water	212° F	100° C	
Bake	325° F	160° C	3
	350° F	180° C	4
	375° F	190° C	5
	400° F	200° C	6
	425° F	220° C	7
	450° F	230° C	8
Broil			Grill